A GUIDE TO PREACHING

SPCK International Study Guides

The SPCK International Study Guides incorporate the much loved and respected TEF series. Written by scholars with experience of the worldwide Church, they combine good scholarship with clarity, simplicity and non-technical language. Ecumenical in authorship and outlook, the Guides are ideal for first-year theology students, Bible study groups, multi-cultural classes, people for whom English is a second language, and anyone who needs a sound but accessible guide to the Bible and theology.

SPCK International Study Guide 38

A GUIDE TO PREACHING

ROGER BOWEN
with
David L. Edwards, David Gitari,
Siméa Meldrum, Esther Mombo
and
Vinoth Ramachandra

First published in Great Britain in 2005

Society for Promoting Christian Knowledge
36 Causton Street
London SW1P 4ST
www.spckpublishing.co.uk

The publisher and author acknowledge with thanks permission to reproduce
extracts from the following:
Eliot, T. S., 'Little Gidding' from *Four Quartets: Collected Poems 1909–62*,
Faber and Faber, reprinted with their permission and that of Harcourt Inc.

Every effort has been made to acknowledge fully the sources of material reproduced in
this book. The publisher apologizes for any omissions that may remain and, if notified,
will ensure that full acknowledgements are made in a subsequent edition.

Scripture quotations from the New Revised Standard Version of the Bible are copyright
© 1989 by the Division of Christian Education of the National Council of the Churches
of Christ in the USA. Used by permission. All rights reserved.

British Library Cataloguing-in-Publication Data
A catalogue record for this book is available from the British Library

ISBN 978–0–281–05726–9

3 5 7 9 10 8 6 4

Typeset by Graphicraft Limited, Hong Kong
First printed in Great Britain at the
University Press, Cambridge

Produced on paper from sustainable forests

CONTENTS

USING THIS GUIDE

This Guide contains practical guidance about preparing and preaching sermons, usually in the normal services of the Church. It also discusses some of the basic principles of preaching, using examples from the Bible, from church history and from many different parts of the world. Differences between cultures show up most in preaching, so readers will find some of the examples and suggestions more helpful than others. This will often depend both on your own culture and also on the culture in which you are preaching.

Some *Special Notes* are included, to deal with specific issues which closely relate to the ministry of preaching.

Study Suggestions at the end of each chapter are designed to help readers to think about the material in that chapter. Readers are encouraged to give their own ideas, either in agreement or in disagreement with what has been written. It may be helpful if some of this reflection is done in small discussion groups. In particular, readers should discuss these issues in relation to sermons which they have heard or preached themselves. Many of the suggestions will remind the reader of actual sermons, either those found in the Guide, or those which readers have experienced. Readers should select the Study Suggestions which seem to be most helpful for their own situation – do not attempt to answer every question in depth.

The *Key to Study Suggestions* will not give an answer to every question. Many questions have no agreed answers – it may be a matter of personal opinion or experience. In some cases the Key directs readers to pages in the Guide where an answer may be found, or to other ways in which they can discover answers for themselves.

The Bible version used in this Guide is the *New Revised Standard Version* (NRSV), which is often used for theological study. This does not imply that it is the best version to use either in preaching or in reading in Church. There are two references to the KJV – the King James (or Authorized) Version.

The *Bibliography* at the end of this Guide is in two parts. The first part lists recommended books on preaching. The second lists all the books and journal articles from which quotations in the text of the Guide have been taken. This series of International Study Guides has not in the past used footnotes or references of this kind, but some serious students may wish to follow up, in their own studies, the issues they have been reading about. References will help them to do this. The references in the text have the form: (Author, date of book:page number), e.g. Gitari, 1996:100 refers to page 100 of David Gitari's book in the bibliography, published in 1996, *In Season and out of Season*.

ACKNOWLEDGEMENTS

I received a good deal of assistance while I was compiling this book. Many of the ideas are not my own, and I have sought to acknowledge them all properly. My qualification for writing this Guide is not my expertise, but rather my experience of listening to sermons in many different cultures.

My heartfelt thanks to the following friends who, in the midst of many heavy pressures, have found time to make material available to me:

> The Most Revd Dr David Gitari, formerly Archbishop of Kenya and a courageous prophet for justice and champion of the poor in that country;
>
> Dr Esther Mombo, currently Academic Dean at St Paul's United Theological College, Limuru, Kenya, whose special gifts are much treasured by the wider Church;
>
> The Revd Siméa Meldrum, who with her husband Ian has for many years shared herself and her family unstintingly with the poor in the *favelas* of Recife, Brazil;
>
> Dr Vinoth Ramachandra, of Sri Lanka, whose ground-breaking writing on global mission has brought new insight and refreshing ideas to us all.
>
> The Very Revd Dr David Edwards has graciously allowed me to adapt a recent article of his, which appears here as Special Note E.

I am indebted to two of my former colleagues at St John's College, Nottingham – Dr John Goldingay, for his contributions especially to Chapter 6, on interpreting the Bible for the pulpit; and Dr Francis Bridger for leading me to Max Atkinson's thought-provoking book and to many of the examples contained in Chapter 5. I thank the editors of *Transformation* for permission to use the article by David Gitari and Ben Knighton in the issue of October 2001, and SCM Press for permission to use Karl Barth's sermon from *Deliverance to the Captives*, 1961, pp. 20–27. I thank Antony Claridge for permitting me to reproduce his sermon in Chapter 9.

The Bibliography names many people upon whose wisdom I have drawn, and there is a particular list of books which readers may find helpful. However, my greatest debt is to generations of students in Africa and Britain to whose sermons I have listened with rapt attention, and many of whom have at times had to listen to mine. In most cases the comments which followed were stimulating and helpful – at least to me.

Much helpful guidance came from Gordon Lamont, and a good deal of hard work from Sally Green, Trisha Dale and colleagues at SPCK. To them all my sincere gratitude.

Wendy, my wife, deserves much sympathy from everyone for having listened to me preaching for many years, and much gratitude from me not only for supplying Special Note C but also for being my best and most constructive critic, of both the spoken and the written word.

INTRODUCTION

Instruction relative to the Composition of Sermons is of great importance, not only to Ministers but, eventually, to the community at large. And it were much to be wished that more regard were paid to this in the education of those who are intended for the ministry.

Charles Simeon, *Horae Homileticae*, vol 1, 1832

The purpose of this Study Guide is to help readers to understand what preaching is and to take practical steps towards preparing and delivering sermons.

Just as a baby learns to crawl before walking, so it is important for preachers to learn the basic skills of preaching before they can develop the special skills of interacting with their hearers, as some of the most famous public speakers in history have done. In Chapters 4 and 5 we shall look at some of those skills. But first, in Chapters 1 and 2, we shall focus our attention on the basic steps necessary in preparing a sermon that expounds Scripture (see pp. 4–5) in a way which is relevant to the hearers. This is called 'expository preaching'. There are other sorts of sermons (see p. 97), most of which are not so easy to preach. In any case, it is good always to anchor the sermon in a Bible passage, for reasons given in Chapter 1.

Most of this Guide is therefore an attempt to give guidelines for preaching expository sermons in Sunday services in church. These are only guidelines. There are no fixed rules for preachers. Preaching cannot be learned through reading this, or any other, book or from attending lectures. All preachers possess their own gifts and cultural experiences of life. For example, Africans often tell vivid stories, and Indians may be gifted at presenting truth through drama. Latin Americans may be better at 'doing' theology in practice than at explaining it. Western Christians have often received special training, which equips them to analyse and expound Scripture in logical and systematic ways. Women often preach differently from men. Sometimes a particular group creates a new art-form. This happened when the early Church produced 'Gospels', which were designed to make the story of Jesus' life a present reality for the readers. It happened when Afro-American slaves sang new songs with music drawn from their African background, but actually forged by the pain of labour in the cotton and sugar plantations and their hope in the gospel. This is why this Guide is written by many different contributors, from a variety of backgrounds.

It would be wrong to force any preacher to adopt a fixed pattern or someone else's style. The England cricket team recently had a fast bowler called Devon Malcolm. He was criticized by one England coach on the grounds that he had 'only one asset – pace', and lacked other skills, such as direction, length and swing. But he bowled the cricket ball so fast and unpredictably that the batsmen often did not know how to play him. If he had been taught to bowl as the coach wanted, he would have been far less effective. In the same way, preachers should be encouraged to use the gifts God has given them, and not made to preach according to some pattern prescribed in a textbook.

Many books on preaching have been written, most of them by Westerners for Western preachers. However, the main strength and vitality of the Christian Church now lies in the continents of Africa, Asia and Latin America, as Philip Jenkins has shown in his recent book, *The Next Christendom*. In the words of one reviewer, this book 'presents a compelling – if sobering – picture of global trends for Christians to ponder'. I would not use the word 'sobering'; I would say 'exciting', because the churches of 'the South' can teach today's preachers in 'the North' how to communicate. Many preachers in the West produce clever, balanced, well-crafted sermons – but they often fail to touch the big issues of daily life. In Britain there are thousands of believing Christians who rarely attend church because they find the preaching boring and irrelevant. It is not like that in the growing churches of the South. That is why they have a ministry to the whole world, and why this book is full of contributions and examples from preachers of the South.

Although this Guide teaches that sermons should always aim to expound the Scriptures, there is no doubt that preachers in those parts of the world where God is reviving and renewing his Church seem to rely more on an imaginative interpretation of the biblical text than an academic exegesis, more on the Holy Spirit than on books, and more on interaction with their audience than on a monologue. This is, in fact, what Jesus did and 'the common people heard him gladly'. We therefore need to learn from them if people are to be attracted to Jesus.

But this book can only suggest some of the ways of learning to preach. The best way of all is through friendly and constructive conversation about what you or someone else has actually said in a sermon. This Guide contains some suggestions about how to do this.

1

APPROACHING THE SERMON

I preached as never sure to preach again,
and as a dying man to dying men.
Richard Baxter, *The Reformed Pastor*, 1656

An academic study of preaching would probably begin by asking the question, 'What is a sermon?' Then it might offer various definitions and review other, more modern means of communication – and only then begin to discuss how to construct a sermon. However, many readers of this Guide probably find themselves wondering how they are going to prepare to preach a sermon next Sunday. So we will start there. When we have considered how to solve this immediate problem, we shall then be in a better position to stand back and analyse what we have been doing.

Preachers often talk about 'writing' the Sunday sermon. This is, however, a misleading word to use. As Martin Luther King Jr wrote, when people asked him if they could publish his sermons, 'A sermon is not an essay to be read but a discourse to be heard . . . directed towards the listening ear rather than the reading eye' (King, 1969:7). Some preachers find it useful to have a fully written script in their hands before they preach; others find that a written script gets in the way of their direct communication with the listeners. Those who have been trained in Western academic theology often feel safer if they have a written script, but there is a danger that they may fall into the trap of writing it as if it were an essay or assignment. If they do, that is what it will sound like – dull and boring. If you do write a script, get into the habit of reading it out loud, preferably to a friend – then you will be writing for speaking, not for reading. Avoid subordinate clauses, use concrete language, don't worry about accurate grammar (see p. 26).

It is better to think in terms of 'preparing' a sermon, for there is far more to preparation than writing, as we shall see. 'Preparing' is not easier than writing; on the contrary, it often requires both perspiration and inspiration as we struggle both with the Bible text and with the needs of our hearers.

3

The Text

Preachers should have a good idea of the text and the topic of their sermon at least a week before preaching it. The text may come to mind on the Sunday beforehand. The text (whether short or long, one word, one verse or a whole chapter) is the essential foundation. Christian preachers are called to serve the word of God, not to pass on their private opinions. 'The gospel that was proclaimed by me,' wrote Paul, 'is not of human origin; for I did not receive it from a human source, nor was I taught it, but I received it through a revelation of Jesus Christ' (Galatians 1.11–12). And the Thessalonians accepted God's message 'not as a human word but as what it really is, God's word, which is also at work in you' (1 Thessalonians 2.13). This is the conviction which lies behind this Guide, and which the preacher should share. God is the subject who is speaking; I am the object, overhearing what he has said. But I can make mistakes, so I need to pray that I shall understand and be receptive. 'This does not lie in our power but only in God's,' wrote Karl Barth. 'This is why prayer must have the last word' (Barth, 1956:1/2, 531).

When you first approach the text, long before you open any books, try to live in it. Let it work on your imagination. Jot down your first impressions and responses – for the congregation is very likely to react to the text in the same way as you do. During this initial period of engaging with the text, be aware also of what is going on around you, both in your local community and in the wider world. You may well discover surprising links. This is not a specific activity in your study; it is a process which stays with you through the week. It will soon become a habit – and even an addiction. You will long to go eagerly to the text to discover what God wants to say to you and then through you to others.

This is important because it is primarily our imagination that makes the link between the ancient text and our present situation. Imagination takes us from what the text meant then to what it means now. Our aim is to preach from what we have discovered in our conversation with the text – and with God. Then we shall want to share our discoveries with others, and say, 'Come on, I've got something to show you!'

But how does the preacher choose a text? Many churches use a regular lectionary of readings with a fresh theme for every Sunday, following the Church's year – in which case the preacher will usually select from those readings.

Other churches set a teaching plan with a series of topics or consecutive texts for a period of time. For example, a local church may plan a series of morning sermons on the seven 'signs' or the 'I am' sayings of Jesus in John's Gospel, or on the parables in Luke, or perhaps 20 consecutive sermons going through Ephesians from beginning to end. For a preaching plan working through Romans, see Cranfield, 1998. Such themes as these are usually selected by the ministry team – or, even better, by the congregation themselves – because they focus on a particular pastoral need recognized within the congregation or within society.

A Nairobi city pastor found that most of the couples coming to be married in the church were very confused about the meaning and principles of Christian marriage. It was obvious that this was a problem not just for them but for most Christians in Nairobi. Very little teaching was ever given about this practical matter, except at weddings, when the problems had either already been solved or would appear only at some future date. Therefore the team planned a series of five sermons on 'The Family' for consecutive Sunday mornings (see p. 15).

Some preachers like to feel that they are being directly led by the Holy Spirit to a particular text or theme for that place on that day. This, however, is very rare. Most preachers prefer to be given some human guidance or even to be told what the theme of the service is to be. Deciding what to preach about can be a harder task than deciding what to say.

Sometimes events of the week demand to be included as a major part of the sermon. The minds of the hearers are on those events, and if preachers talk about something else, then they will not command attention and they may as well not preach at all. On 21 March 1980 there was a total eclipse of the sun in Kenya, and all over the country on 23 March preachers referred to that eclipse, which everyone had experienced. In Nairobi Cathedral, the sermon was about 2 Corinthians 3.12–18, and the way in which the Sun of Righteousness (Christ) shines on people when the veil of sin and ignorance is removed. He produces the fruit of the Spirit, just as the sun shines brightly after the eclipse to bring forth various fruits of the earth. But different fruit is produced in different climates. Pineapples do not grow in Sweden so have to be imported; in the same way, people of different cultures have developed different gifts. They all come from God, so people need to 'import' help from one another to serve him effectively.

On another occasion, a preacher found on his arrival at the church that a member of the youth fellowship had been knifed to death the day before. This made it impossible to preach his prepared sermon, so he modified it to meet the grief and despair of the people at that time. Diana, Princess of Wales was killed in a car crash early on Sunday

31 August 1997, and many preachers that day changed their sermons at the very last minute – for she was 'the people's princess'.

John Wesley, the great English preacher of the eighteenth century, believed that every time he preached he was taking part in a drama of which God was the Director. It was God who was bringing preacher and hearers together to communicate a message specially suited to that particular situation and set of circumstances. Once Wesley was facing a mob of rioting coal miners who gradually quietened down and were touched by the message. Another day he was violently robbed of all his money as he was riding his horse from one town to another – but he warned the robber that God would meet with him that very night and lay claim to his soul, and so it turned out. If we are to think like that, we must first of all be servants of God's word, not our own ideas. Second, we must believe that God's Spirit is in control of all the circumstances that we meet. Then we shall be likely to see how God is at work in ways beyond our control.

It is important normally to use the Bible version which is most familiar to the listeners, even though we may refer to other translations to help them understand the meaning of the text. Some texts are best avoided, such as those in the following categories:

1 Texts that are so well known that you cannot find anything new to say about them.
2 Difficult texts, which raise in people's minds bigger problems than you can solve.
3 A group of three or four texts that happen to be together in the lectionary but otherwise bear no obvious relation to one another. It is better to select one of the texts and expound it in its own biblical context, so that it speaks to people in the way the original writer intended. See Special Note A, p. 34.
4 A text that is too short to reflect the original writer's intention and standpoint.
5 As a normal rule, topics (e.g. prayer, the atonement) should also be avoided. When pastors begin their preaching ministry, they often try to cover topics, but find that they soon run dry. Colin Morris writes that he used to preach on 'subjects', but he soon ran out of subjects because he was trying to say too much in one sermon. 'Once I reverted to preaching from biblical texts, I found I had an inexhaustible mine of rich material' (1996:67).

Please note that these are warnings for the beginner. Through long experience, preachers learn how to handle well-known texts, difficult texts and combinations of texts and topics.

The Context

Every text has a context. This means that it forms part of a logical argument, or story, or situation. When preaching, we need to take account of even wider contexts than these. The contexts are often of even more importance than the text, so we must now consider these.

The Biblical Context

When the Gospel writers composed their Gospels about the life of Jesus, they were aware of at least three, and sometimes four, separate contexts:

1 The situation in the life of Jesus – that is, the needs or questions of the people to whom he was speaking; the religious and social world in which they lived; the ideas they held; and the part which this incident played in his overall ministry.
2 The situation in the lives of Jesus' followers and those who heard them. Why did they remember these events, talk about them and pass them on to other believers – and even unbelievers – as they went about preaching? They created the 'oral tradition' out of which our New Testament came to be written. So what was their situation, which made this story important to them in the 30 years after the death of Jesus (before the Gospels were written down)?
3 The life and situation of the Gospel writer and the people – perhaps his friends in his own church – for whom he was writing. Why did he select this particular story from all the stories he knew? Why, out of all the miracles which Jesus did, were the seven signs that John chose specially significant? Why did Luke take the incident of Jesus' rejection by his own people at Nazareth, which seems to have taken place in the middle of his Galilean ministry (Mark 6.1–6), and place it right at the beginning of Jesus' ministry (Luke 4.16–30)? The writers had their own very good reasons for writing as they did, and preachers must be aware of these, if they are to expound the word properly.
4 Finally, most of the writers of the New Testament were aware of the Jewish Scriptures, which were their Bible. Their reading and understanding of those Scriptures was an important part of their context, and modern preachers need to recognize this.

For example, anyone preaching on the feeding of the five thousand in John 6 should take account of the following facts (Newbigin, 1982:73):

1 Jesus interpreted this miracle as a sign of the fact that he had been sent by the Father to be the bread of life for all who believe in him.
2 Jesus' hearers knew how God had miraculously fed their ancestors in the desert.

3 This story was recalled in many of the oral traditions about Jesus (see Mark 6.30–52; 8.1–21; Matthew 14.13–33; 15.32–9; Luke 9.10–22).

4 John and his readers would certainly have made a connection between this story and their regular experience of meeting together at the Eucharist to eat bread and drink wine in memory of Jesus' death for them on the cross.

5 John understood Jesus' death, which took place on the eve of the Passover festival, to be the sacrifice which established the new covenant between God and his people.

The theological discipline of 'form criticism' (see p. 11) can help us with this, but it is important to note that this work should be done in the preacher's workshop – in preparation for preaching. It is not necessary to explain it to the congregation. A carpenter brings out a finished table for his customers to see; he does not show them the tools he used in making it, but without the tools he would not have been able to make such a fine table. And he draws on years of practice. In the same way preachers must try to be abreast of modern culture and theology – if not, they will soon run out of ideas and begin to be repetitive.

Remember that the context may well be as fruitful as the text. For example, are Christians comforted or challenged by Jesus' story of the two men who went up to the Temple to pray (Luke 18.9–14), or by the episode of the elder son in the parable of the Two Lost Sons (Luke 15.11–32)? These two stories were shocking to religious people of Jesus' time, but we need to know the context if we are to understand this – and especially if these ancient stories are to be as effective today as they were to those who listened to Jesus. See pp. 106–7.

Preachers must learn to hear their texts with exactly the shade of meaning they had for the first writer or readers. They need to study the language, culture and history of the time, the mood (anger, grief, joy) of the text, and the theology of each writer. Favourite themes of Luke, for example, were the Holy Spirit, joy, women's lives and Jerusalem. The different insights of the various authors of the Bible ensure that sermons need never be colourless or predictable. Passages of Scripture present mysteries in order to explain them, or describe danger to arouse interest in the rescue, or portray a tense crisis followed by its resolution – and that is exactly what preachers can do in their sermons.

The Personal Context

The Preacher

Preachers must be aware of their own present situation and their past experiences, for these factors are bound to affect how they think and what they say. On the one hand preachers should not reflect themselves and their agenda, but instead the agenda of the word of God and the needs of the people. On the other hand, the preacher is a fellow-pilgrim with the congregation and needs to show that the message is as much for the preacher as for the hearers, partly by saying 'we' as much as 'you'. You may identify with one of the characters in the story – but be careful you do not always make yourself the hero! You might, for example, be not the father but the elder son in Luke 15.28, sulking and jealous. Henri Nouwen imagines in his book *The Return of the Prodigal Son* what it feels like to be each of the characters of that story in turn. The most effective sermons have touched the emotions of the preacher before they touch the congregation. The preacher is not only a messenger but also a witness (Kurewa, 2000:114). The way people respond to a sermon is very often governed by how they respond to the personality of the preacher.

It is sometimes said that you cannot preach about what you have not experienced. This is only partly true. People who are not married can preach about marriage (often very well, as wise observers from the outside), and the best sermons about dying are preached by those who have not yet died! In any case, the preacher is never alone, but has 2,000 years' experience of fellow-Christians to draw from. Many of them have written vividly about their experiences, and they are part of the preacher's resources today. But our own experiences, while they are fascinating to us, may be boring and irrelevant to our hearers. A mother loves to tell stories about her children, but the congregation will not share her interest. Students at theological college often illustrate their sermons with their own experience of the lecture room, the college community or even of preparing this sermon! These matters are neither interesting nor relevant to the congregation, so preachers must learn to be ruthless in cutting such things out of their sermons.

The Listeners

The situation of the listeners is even more important, and will sometimes determine the text, theme and content of the sermon. One Friday in March 1987 a big steamer, *Herald of Free Enterprise*, capsized in the English Channel. Over 100 people died, and many were dramatically rescued. On the Saturday millions of people were sitting in front of their TV sets watching the drama unfold. No one preaching in the UK on the Sunday could afford to be silent about that event – for it was uppermost in everyone's mind that day. The assassinations of President John Kennedy, of Martin Luther King Jr, of Mahatma Gandhi and of Mrs Indira Gandhi were events which come into the same category. If we cannot preach the word of God relevantly to our hearers, it will be better to keep quiet.

One day in a small village church a student was preaching about suffering. He used examples of minor sicknesses being healed and of discomforts being endured. But sitting in a wheelchair in the front row of the congregation was a quadriplegic fellow-student who since birth had been unable to control his physical movements or do anything for himself except hear, see, think and, with difficulty, speak. Everyone was thinking about his suffering as the preacher went on about how God can cure minor aches and pains. The real preacher in that church was the disabled man, who said nothing! He should have been the text on which the student preached; how powerful it would have been.

In some countries, TV dramas called 'soap operas' are viewed by millions. In the 1980s there were 19 million British people watching *EastEnders* twice every week, all about the lives of ordinary Londoners – and very much like the lives of the viewers themselves, which is why they were so interested. Preachers who use those stories from local soap operas in their sermons can be sure of people's interest and understanding.

The only way to preach biblically is to pay serious attention to the situation of the listeners. That is what Jesus always did. Repeatedly he responded to what he heard, rather than teaching ready-made lessons. Writers in the Bible adapted and modified the tradition they had received to fit the situation, or meet the needs, or address the questions faced by them and their readers. This does not mean that they altered the words of their teacher, which had been handed down to them as sacred tradition. Like all pupils of Jewish rabbis, they were faithful to the original meaning. But when situations and cultures change, so do meanings. John, for example, included in his Gospel much imagery, poetry and typology [interpretation of symbols] which are not found in Mark, who was more prosaic. In practice, all readers automatically make adjustments like this when they read the sacred texts that are important for their life. We apply it to our own lives today, and the Bible encourages us to do just that.

The Church Context

Preachers should always ask, 'What happened this time last week in this church?', for that is where the people were, whether the preacher was there or not. Does this church have a continuous teaching programme? Does it follow the church year, or a special lectionary? Has anything been said or done recently in this church on the topic I am going to deal with? What are the main pastoral and teaching needs of the people here? Is there a bookstall? If so, what sort of books does it have? Is there a simple book on the theme of my sermon that I can recommend?

The church building can be very informative to the preacher. If you are to preach in a church for the first time, it is a good idea to pay a visit beforehand – ideally on the Sunday before you are due to preach, if possible. Sermon preparation is much easier if you have a mental picture of the building. Buildings affect people, and they certainly affect sermons! A sermon style that is suitable for a huge, 1,000-year-old European cathedral will sound quite out of place in a new village church in Papua New Guinea. Many churches have ancient inscriptions or modern notices, which can inform the preacher and even illustrate the sermon. Local illustrations are always the best. See p. 65 for some examples.

The Liturgical Context

Do not imagine that people come to church to hear you preach. It may be the big event for you, but not for them. They come for worship, prayer and fellowship. It is therefore essential that the sermon blends in with the Scripture readings, the hymns, the prayers, the choir songs – even the notices. Preachers need to pay careful attention to every part of the service and link the sermon with what has gone before. A service which hangs together in this way will certainly make an impact on the worshippers, for it will all work together to support the theme. It will also make them realize, 'The preacher is interested in us and in our lives.' A sermon that stands alone will be criticized alone, just as if it is a one-person performance – which a true sermon should never be.

Text and Context: How They Interact

We have already noted that every Scripture text had a context, both of writer and of readers. The theological discipline of 'redaction criticism' asks, 'What were the *interests of this particular author* which led him to include this particular text?' We need to understand in what ways those interests were similar to our interests today, and in what ways they were different. 'Form criticism' asks, 'What were the *needs and questions of the people* who received this tradition which made the author set it down in this particular way?' Many of their interests and questions were probably rather like those of people today. 'Should we pay taxes to [Rome] a foreign, colonial government?' is a question which has been asked by Palestinians in Jerusalem, by Muslims in Bosnia and by Hutus in Rwanda in modern times. Not many people today ask questions about sabbath observance, as the people of Jesus' time did, but in Northern Nigeria, for example, they ask questions about other religious laws which are imposed on them. And most people ask questions about marriage, divorce and human sexuality like those we find in the Gospels.

All over the world, people want to know more about Jesus and how he is relevant for their lives. The miracle stories in the Gospels gave their first readers the answer in forms which they could easily remember, for the benefit of both themselves and their friends. Often the Church has spoken more about its laws, its priests, its buildings and its rituals than about Jesus. Preaching on the texts in the contexts of the Gospels can help people to see Jesus again in the light of their own problems, just as the Gospel writers did in their own time.

We need to understand the context of our hearers even more than that of the original readers. One evangelist was preparing to lead a town mission, and was invited to spend a day or two going on a tour of the town, to learn more about the people who lived there. He declined, saying, 'Their situation will not have any effect on the message I bring.' A teacher in a theological college said he would not attend a student seminar on his lectures, 'because', he said, 'nothing they say will affect what I say in my lectures'. These two people were running the risk of spending a lot of time answering questions which nobody was asking. They 'knew' what they had to say before they looked at the situation. They were content with 'a mere recitation of the traditional word of God in which the word of God does not enter language in the present' (Ebeling, 1961:184). 'He, the listener, is my theme,' wrote Ernst Lange (Runia, 1983:61). The late Bishop Festo Kivengere, the great Ugandan evangelist, before accepting an invitation to preach, used to ask, 'If you have something as your concern, share it with me, it will help me as I pray.' The gospel cannot be preached apart from what the people who hear it are themselves struggling with. See p. 43.

This is the pattern adopted by all writers in the New Testament. They preached to Gentiles in a different way from Jews. Paul was able to use the philosophical methods of the Athenian marketplace, or the Gnostic language of Colosse, or the imagery of the Jewish Scriptures. It depended on who he was speaking to. Jesus talked with Galilean peasants differently from the way he argued with religious leaders in Jerusalem. The thought and language of John's Gospel differs from that of Luke. Preachers who use the same forms for all audiences are not following the biblical model.

It is true that the basic elements of the good news never change, since they are founded upon God's action in Jesus Christ and through the Holy Spirit. However, the scope of the good news is so wide that it embraces not only eternal salvation but also healing, liberating, feeding, relating, resting – all those blessings which Jesus brought with him to those he met. Therefore I cannot know precisely what the good news is for people until I get to know them. The Roman Catholic missionary, Vincent Donovan, wrote that the result of his meeting with the Masai people of Tanzania was that 'they and I went together to a place where neither of us had been before' (Donovan, 1978:vii). When anyone brings the message of salvation to new people, both sides discover more of what that message means to them, the preacher as much as the hearer.

We do not know exactly what problems were facing the various recipients of the letters of the New Testament – but we can discover more about them by reading those letters, because the letters were 'contextual' and spoke to the situation. That is why they are all different. We ought always to ask the same question about our sermons. Are they so relevant that, years later, someone could discover the situation of our hearers through reading them?

Klaas Runia wrote:

> The living Word of God always occurs *at the point of intersection* of the message of the text with the concrete situation of those who hear the message. Today too, the message of Scripture becomes fruitful for preaching only when the minister, in solidarity with his congregation, tries to accomplish this intersecting. How he has to do this he does not know beforehand. (1983:65)

Runia then identified two faulty methods of sermon preparation and proposed a third method:

1 The *traditional* method: to carefully examine the text and then try to apply it to the lives of the congregation. 'He dumps it off at the pews.' This is one-way traffic.

2 The *situational* method is the opposite. Starting with the questions of the hearers, the preacher searches through the Bible to find some relevant answers to those questions. This method limits the Bible to answering our questions and misses the important questions which the Bible puts to us, which we would never have thought of by ourselves.

3 The *interactive* method is better. It has six stages:

First, always start with the biblical text, for God's Word is primary.

Second, try to see the text through the eyes of the hearers – how will they respond? with understanding or misunderstanding? with joy or resistance? and why? The reason will probably be found in the prevailing culture or world-view. Does the Bible challenge this, or approve of it?

Third, go back to the text and search for the original message of the writer, now bearing in mind the likely reactions of the hearers.

Fourth, now relate the original message to these reactions. Maybe it will answer their questions; maybe it will ask them a different question; maybe it will criticize them; maybe it will support them. And maybe it will seem to have nothing to do with their situation, and in that case the preacher may have to carry the text on until it does. Jesus (or his hearers) often did this by adding a bit extra to a story he told, e.g. Mt. 22.11–13; Lk. 10.37; 15.25–32.

Fifth, now write down the aim of your sermon.
Finally, work on the details of the whole sermon.

Those who follow this discipline will find that the hearers get personally involved in the sermon, as the text begins to engage with their situation and their own feelings. This is the normal experience of people conversing with one another, or watching a TV programme about something that interests them. Very soon someone interrupts to comment on what is being said. Some who are watching want people to be quiet, so that they can listen to the discussion; others want to express their opinion so much that they cannot keep quiet. If a preacher is really communicating, this is what will happen in the congregation – they will want to start talking about it themselves. That is what preaching is.

The science of preaching is called 'homiletics', which comes from the Greek verb *homileo*, converse. Perhaps preachers should be pleased if people start chatting during the sermon, especially if they are discussing the topic of the sermon. If they are discussing something else, it is probably because they find the sermon irrelevant. Paul expected people to discuss his letters as they listened to them being read out at church meetings. In fact, he could well imagine what they were likely to say, so he anticipated it in his letter – see Romans 3.1–8; 6.1; 9.14, 19. He knew people would be interested because he had taken the trouble to connect his text with their context. When this is done, it always results in dialogue.

The Theme

Once you have spent some time thinking about the text and the different contexts, you will begin to have a theme in your mind. Sometimes (e.g. at a funeral or marriage, or on Good Friday) you know the theme of the sermon long before you decide on a text. One verse can contain a number of different themes. John 3.16 is a good example, which is one reason why it is not an easy verse to preach on. A sermon should have only one theme, but may approach it from a number of different angles, all of which throw light on the one theme and reinforce the one aim. A Bible exposition is different, for it needs to include all the themes present in the text, but will probably not discuss or apply them in such depth.

On the other hand, some themes are so central to faith or to life that it is necessary to deal with them not in one sermon, but in many, perhaps in a planned series. For example, you may consider the resurrection of Christ in one sermon as a past, historical event; in another as the present experience of believers who now share new life in Christ;

and in yet another to encourage Christians to look forward to the future hope of resurrection. These could be given three titles: 'The Resurrection of Christ'; 'Resurrection in Christ'; 'Resurrection like Christ'. The sermon series on the family mentioned on p. 5 could have five parts relating closely to human life and experience, as follows:

1 God's Plan for Marriage and Family (Genesis 2.22–4);
2 How to Choose a Life Partner (Genesis 29);
3 Husbands and Wives Together (Ephesians 5.21–33);
4 Children and their Parents (Ephesians 6.1–4);
5 God's Human Family (Mark 3.31–5).

It will help the congregation if the pastor announces the theme at the beginning of the service, and then ensures that all parts of the service – hymns, readings, prayers, etc. – are built round that theme. Try to make the theme sound interesting. If the theme is the transfiguration of Jesus, why not call it 'Jesus gives us a glimpse of his true self'? Or, on Luke 12.16–21, 'Your money or your life'. Ephesians 4.7–16 might be called, 'What's wrong with our church?' The theme will reflect the 'big idea', sometimes called the 'motif' of the text, and it will relate to the aim – what does God want us to understand and do?

Study Suggestions

1 In John 6, which verses reflect each of the five themes mentioned on pp. 7–8? See also parallel passages in Matthew, Mark and Luke, and see John 13.1.
2 Which aspect of the parable of the Two Lost Sons (Luke 15.11–32) do you feel would be most relevant for the Christian community you belong to? Why?
3 Mention three issues of topical interest today in the community where you live. What ought the church to be saying about each one?
4 Think of two questions answered by Jesus which people of today might want to ask.
5 Select any two New Testament letters, and name a significant problem faced by the recipients, which we can deduce from the contents of the letters.
6 If you were preaching on Philippians 2.5–11, what would the aim of your sermon be? What other aim might you have? What was Paul's purpose when he wrote it?
7 Describe any congregational reaction to a sermon which you have noticed in your experience. Why did they react in that way?
8 What are the main differences between a sermon and a Bible exposition?

2

BUILDING THE SERMON

Our parson can preach as good a sermon as need be heard when he writes it down. But when he tries to preach without a book, he rambles about and doesn't stick to his text; and every now and then he flounders about like a sheep that has cast itself and can't stand up.

George Eliot, *Scenes of Clerical Life*, 1858

A good sermon is one people listen to; a bad sermon is one they don't. Getting and holding attention is the name of the game.

David Winter, *Church Times*, 24 August 2001

The Process

We have seen enough in Chapter 1 to realize that preparing a sermon focuses on two processes. The first is to uncover the message contained in the biblical text. The second is to communicate that message. The two processes are distinct but closely related. For example, the form of the text should determine the form of the communication. Both processes involve the preacher in a journey of discovery; and preachers will not be able to think about the meaning of a text without thinking about the situation of the people they are going to bring it to. But we should still be clear about the fact that there are two processes, not one. At some point, after 'hearing' the message of the text, the preacher should go off and think about something quite different, before returning to grapple with the bigger process of 'translating' it into the thought-forms of the congregation.

Ramesh Richard, from New Delhi, in his book *Scripture Sculpture* describes this twofold process as *exegesis* (comment on the meaning of the text as originally written) and *exposition* (interpretation of the text for today's readers), and as two contexts: then and now. He pictures it as the study of a figure and the carving of a statue. Some readers may find his diagram a helpful way of describing this process in seven distinct steps, as shown in Figure 2.1.

Richard shows how working first on the biblical text and then upon the sermon leads the preacher from the initial study of the text to the

1 Study the text (flesh)　　　　　　　7 Preach the sermon (flesh)
2 The Structure of the text (skeleton)　　6 The Structure of the sermon (skeleton)
3 The Big Idea of the text (heart)　　　　5 The Big Idea of the sermon (heart)

　　　　　　　　　　4 The Purpose Bridge (brain)

Figure 2.1 The twofold process

final delivery of the sermon. He rightly regards Step 4 as the crucial step in the work of preparation, because this is where the link is made between the ancient text and the world of today. Further attention is given to this topic in Chapter 6.

The Congregation

You have got your text, you have got your theme, you have considered the situation of the congregation. Now it is necessary to think about your hearers in more detail. What questions, memories, pains and problems do they have? Will these be stirred up by this sermon? Will the sermon encourage them to face issues, or will it drive them into depression? A sermon preached about family life in an African city church drew this response from a young woman as she left the service: 'Why do you put such an ideal situation before us? It is a mockery. Family life like that is for ever beyond my reach. With these three little children (all with different fathers), who will ever marry me now? There is no way back for me!'

Is that true? Is there no way back? Of course there is, always, but the preacher had not said so, and she was in despair. It was really important, on the following Sunday, for the preacher to speak of how God welcomes everyone into his own family. The woman had said what she was thinking, but for every one person who does that, there are 99 who suffer in silence. So preachers must use their imagination to put themselves in the shoes of all those who may listen to them.

If the majority of the congregation come from one country, tribe or class, it may be unwise to use an illustration which arouses people's emotions about a country, tribe or class towards which they have felt hostile. Your illustration may be an excellent one, but if it is going to help the hearers it needs to be adapted so that it will not unnecessarily stir up any deeply felt emotions.

The preacher needs to be fully aware of any difficulties or doubts which the sermon will raise – and then either deal with those issues or omit that part of the sermon altogether. The pastor who visits the people of the parish regularly and listens to them is the very best person to do the preaching. Those visits and conversations not only create shared feelings between preacher and people but also supply the best illustrations and raw material for sermons.

One pastor in a rural area complained that it was not worth going on long journeys every Sunday to preach to very small congregations. Then he read about C. H. Spurgeon who, as a teenager, went out on a snowy morning to a little chapel in Colchester. Hardly anyone turned up, and even the preacher failed to arrive. So one of the deacons, who had no training and very little education, stood up and preached a terrible sermon. He kept repeating himself, 'Look to Jesus! Look to Jesus!' Those words, repeated by an ignorant but sincere believer, convinced Spurgeon that he needed to turn to Jesus. Charles Haddon Spurgeon became one of the greatest preachers of all time, attracting congregations of 20,000 people to open-air services in London by the time he was 20 years old and being reported in Monday's newspapers in the USA as well as in the UK. The preacher never knows who may be listening, but the Bible reminds us that a great company of angels is listening intently to those who proclaim the gospel, and they give glory and praise to God for it (Ephesians 3.10; 1 Peter 1.12).

The Aim

You started to think about your sermon on the Sunday or Monday beforehand. You have seen the theme, but by Tuesday evening you should begin to have a clear idea of your aim. Now you must write it down. If you aim at nothing, you will probably achieve nothing. If you have no idea of what effect you want your sermon to have on the lives of your hearers, you can hardly expect them to be clear about it either.

A sermon should have just *one, short, practical* aim. It should be *one*, so that it is simple and clear, not diverting the attention of the hearers to other matters which, though interesting, do not serve the aim. It should be *short*, so that the preacher never loses sight of it in preparation, in preaching or in the pastoral discussions which may follow. It should be *practical*, because Christian faith is practical rather than theoretical. It works in people's lives by altering their attitudes or actions. It can do this by touching their emotions so that they *feel* something, by strengthening their faith so that they *believe* something, or by moving their wills so that they *do* something.

'To teach . . . so that they understand . . . or remember . . .' is not a proper aim. Preaching which affects only people's minds is not Christian preaching. The Greeks were often satisfied when they succeeded in grasping some truth with their minds, but Hebrew – and biblical – thinking is always practical. (One of the problems of the churches

18

in the Western world is that they have been so influenced by Aristotle and the philosophy of the Enlightenment that they are often satisfied with theoretical knowledge.) When we have *understood* something – such as the causes of crime, the methods of irrigation or the reasons for environmental disasters – it is easy to deceive ourselves into thinking that we have solved the problem, when in fact we have done nothing about it. Jesus criticized people who thought like this when he said, 'Why do you call me, Lord, Lord, yet do not the things which I say?' 'The words please you,' said Augustine to his congregation, 'but I want to see actions!' So he ended every sermon with a call to prayer: 'And now let us turn to the Lord' (Brilioth, 1950:7).

One writer made this mistake when he wrote that a clear aim 'enables the hearers (a) to concentrate during the sermon, (b) to remember the sermon and (c) to recount it clearly to others'. This is never the aim of preaching, any more than I eat a good meal in order to remember and talk about it the next day! I eat good food so that I shall be strong and healthy. I eat to live; I do not live to eat! In the same way, I listen to sermons so that I shall be moved and changed. A sermon is to be digested, not remembered. Its future life lies neither in a written text nor in the memory of the congregation. A sermon's real future lies in the response and life of the listeners – and in this way may even change the world.

The distinction between these two kinds of aims is reflected by comparing the aims of Luke and John in writing their Gospels. Luke wrote his Gospel for Theophilus 'so that you may know the truth concerning the things about which you have been instructed', i.e. the events of the life and death of Jesus (Luke 1.4). No doubt Luke wanted Theophilus to believe, but his stated aim was 'apologetic', which means clarifying and defending the truth of the gospel. John's stated aim, on the other hand, was that his readers might 'believe that Jesus is the Messiah, the Son of God, and that through believing you may have life in his name' (John 20.31).

In the end, people don't receive the truth when someone explains it in words, but they do receive it either when they encounter it in their own experience or when they listen in to some drama and 'the penny drops' – the truth dawns upon them. The preacher has to bring about this encounter situation, so that they 'see' it for themselves and find joy or repentance or renewal. Mental understanding is not really 'knowing' unless it is rooted in experience and worked out in practice.

A Bagful of Material

Now write your sermon aim in big letters at the top of a sheet of paper. Then write down underneath all the material you have collected up to now, especially points of contact, relevance, illustrations and thoughts you have had on the text, etc. At the bottom of the page you may wish to write down possible sub-topics, points of exegesis, difficult issues, etc. You will probably discard many of these from this sermon, though some may come in useful on later occasions.

It is worth remembering 'the three Rs' of preaching (Ireson, 1982:33):

1 *Register*: i.e. establish contact with the minds, lives and situations of the hearers;
2 *Reveal*: i.e. open up the truth of the text in such a way that the hearers can see what it means for them today – it 'rings a bell' for them;
3 *Relate*: i.e. show them how they should respond in faith and life so that God's word makes a difference to them.

Registering and relating should normally focus on the situation of the hearers. Revealing should normally focus mainly on the biblical text – though by the time the sermon is preached, the ancient text and the present situation should be interwoven.

Illustrations

The Bible, literature, history, the newspaper, radio, TV, our experiences – all are full of thousands of illustrations and examples which we can use in our preaching. The problem is that most of us find it difficult to bring these to mind when we are actually preparing a sermon. Many in the Western world have got into the bad habit of making a distinction between daily life and the world of religion. Jesus never made this mistake, though many of his opponents did. We need to see life as a whole, not in separate, unconnected compartments.

There are four main purposes in using illustrations.

1 They clarify a point to help the listeners understand it. The preacher may say, 'It is like this . . .' or even 'It is *not* like this . . .', and then give an analogy (comparing one thing with another).
2 They help listeners to concentrate on what the preacher is saying and then reflect on it afterwards.
3 They make the sermon more enjoyable to listen to, like including vegetables, meat or curry in your dish of rice.
4 Examples make listeners want to go out and do the same, i.e. they provoke action.

Chapter 4 will deal with some sorts of illustrations in detail, but we note here one or two common examples. Writers in the Bible constantly used picture-language. Isaiah sang a love-song at his local agricultural show (5.1–7) – but it had a sting in the tail! Amos (1.3—2.8) denounced the atrocities of the nations – but again there was a sting in the tail. Paul used the same technique in Romans 1.18—2.16, but then added 2.17–24. Nathan told King David a story of abuse of human rights which infuriated the king – until he realized that he himself was the abuser (2 Samuel 12.1–7). Hosea and Amos used concrete pictures of marriage, farming and building, so familiar to everyone, to speak of both judgement and mercy.

African, Chinese and Indian cultures all have rich traditions of proverbs and stories which point up some moral lesson. Christians have adapted many of these as illustrations of the gospel. When a proverb or story is well known, preachers can use the technique of starting it off and then letting the people finish it aloud. Or they can begin a story and then ask questions about it for the people to answer. In this way the listeners are involved because the world of the story is familiar to them – and they are likely to be equally involved in applying it to their own lives. The light will dawn upon them more effectively when they see it for themselves than if they are told by the preacher. Jesus did the same. Many of his parables were not new stories but old ones well known to Jewish rabbis (see Bailey, 1983). In the same way Charles Wesley – and in modern times many African musicians – used popular tunes and put Christian words to them. The 'language of the people' is always the best way to communicate with the people.

Choose illustrations which are interesting and relevant to their world. As a general rule, do not talk about things which are unfamiliar to the hearers, or which are for them matters of dispute. Avoid illustrations which are over-complicated, off the point, trivial or unrealistic. Use only sparingly illustrations about your own life and experiences. If you refer to someone else's real-life experience (which can be very helpful), ensure that you never reveal anything which someone has told you in confidence. From time to time a completely unrealistic fable (say, about animals) can be effective (see p. 52).

Christian ministers are often taught to do 'theological reflection', but ordinary people are reflecting theologically all the time – therefore you should take illustrations from the things they are reflecting about. The tragic sinking of the *Herald of Free Enterprise* (see p. 9, above) brought onto the TV screens of the UK a picture of a little girl struggling in the water as a man reached down to rescue her. 'Why do I have to die?' she asked. 'I've been such a good girl.' A pastor could easily preach an effective sermon on a simple thought like this.

Just as the prophets sometimes used dramatic actions to make a vivid point (e.g. Jeremiah 19.1–11), so we can do the same today (see p. 63). A preacher took a broom and swept out the sanctuary in silence while the pianist played Beethoven's 'Rage over a Lost Penny' on the piano. His text, when he came to it, turned out to be Luke 15.8–10. Another minister, preparing to preach on the same text, hid his sermon notes in a Bible in one of the church pews and then pretended that he had lost them. He got everyone in the church thumbing through all the books until someone shouted 'I've found it' – and then he responded, 'Rejoice with me, for I have found the notes that I had lost!' The congregation listened to that sermon!

Keep a notebook of all illustrations, examples, stories, etc., as they occur to you through reading books, listening to the radio, seeing films, talking with friends. Classify them according to the topic which each one illustrates, so that you can look them up when you need an illustration. After ten years of doing this, you will find that you will not need your notebook any more, for the process will come to you naturally.

Stop!

At this point, you may have collected so much material and so many ideas that you are getting confused. It is time to stop. Distance yourself from your preparation. Even try to forget the details of it. Go back to your basic text; quietly meditate and pray over it for a day or two. Focus not on what you are going to say, but on what God is saying to you. This is the most important part of your preparation. Do not hunt for any more ideas for the time being, but keep your eyes and ears open to see what God is doing in the events of the week. Remember that you are an actor in a drama which God is directing (see p. 6). Expect God to continue his work through your sermon, even if it is weak and inadequate, in relation to the real-life events around you. Conduct a three-cornered conversation between those events, yourself and your sermon. You could enlist the help of a friend, or even of a small group, who may have new insights on your topic. If you do this, then you acknowledge that your sermon is not yours alone, but a joint production (as it always is, if we are honest) – it will then carry the extra authority of their combined Christian wisdom.

An English woman pastor, who was conducting a wedding one Saturday, received in the post that very morning a letter from a friend who had gone to work in Africa for a year. He wrote how he and his wife had found renewal in their marriage through this cross-cultural experience. Since one of the couple being married was English and the other Chinese, the pastor quoted from the letter during the wedding ceremony. It seemed that God had provided it specially to help her in her ministry at that moment. We should expect such things to happen, and look out for them.

Teaching

Now it is time to turn to commentaries on your text – and on the context of your text. You may also wish to read theological or practical books which deal with your topic.

Do not read these commentaries before you have gathered your basic thoughts – to do so will distract you from giving proper consideration to the context of your hearers.

Do not read other people's sermons on your text. This is likely to obscure the clarity of your aim, and confuse you and the hearers.

But *do relate* the teaching in your sermon to three things:

1 Your own systematic theology (attempt to arrange your beliefs self-consistently). What Christian doctrine is this sermon meant to illuminate? How does it fit in with our beliefs? Does it create contradictions or problems, and how can I resolve these in a constructive and creative way? See pp. 99–101. Perhaps you cannot resolve them, but perhaps this will not matter. The Bible gives us pictures of real life, which is often untidy and disorderly. The work of the Holy Spirit in Acts, for example, often seems to be unpredictable and unsystematic.
2 The faith and world view of your hearers. For example, what is the point of talking about prayer and 'signs and wonders' if your hearers are convinced that prayer is not answered and that miracles don't happen? In this case they will need a process of faith-education, and probably to have some experience first. Few Tanzanian Christians expected God to heal physical ailments until Brother Edmond John discovered this gift in 1973 and, as a result, the ministry of healing spread throughout the churches.
3 The person and work of Jesus Christ. Every Christian sermon, even on Old Testament texts, must relate somehow to Jesus and his work of salvation for humankind. See p. 31. This need not be done openly throughout the sermon, but can be brought in as an illustration or as a conclusion relating to your aim or chief point.

Use

Puritan preachers in England in the seventeenth century used to have one section of their sermons entitled 'Use', by which they meant: 'how to apply this teaching in daily life'. This means the same as 'relate' (see p. 20). What do I expect my hearers to do in response to this word from God? They will not do anything unless the preacher has first listened so carefully to his own sermon that it has touched and challenged him.

Once a preacher was standing in the pulpit of his own parish church, preaching as usual, when he stopped, silent, unable to say any more. Tears began to run down his cheeks. Suddenly a member of the congregation stood up, raised his arms and shouted, 'Praise the Lord; the parson's been converted!' And so it was; the Revd William Haslam had been converted by his own sermon (Haslam, 1880:48). Then he announced the Doxology ('Praise God from whom all blessings flow . . .'), which everyone sang enthusiastically. That will not happen very often, but something like it should happen every time we preach.

But we must not think that people will respond by doing just what we tell them to. We must be more subtle than that. To explain the meaning of repentance or faith will not make people repent or believe. Only 'seeing' Jesus will make them do that, just as Peter 'saw' Jesus for the first time in Luke 5.8 – and Jesus was able to commission him for service. Or think of the father who in faith had to ask Jesus, 'Help my unbelief' (Mark 9.24).

Therefore we must be careful not to moralize in our sermons. Telling people to 'pray more' or scolding them for their faults is not likely to bring about any lasting change in their lives. It may make them feel guilty for a time. It may make them more religious, but probably not more Christian. Most likely it will make them feel that they have paid the price for their wrongdoing by coming to church on Sunday and getting a good telling-off, and now they can go back to living just as they did before.

This is what Richard Baxter wrote in 1656 about preaching:

> Men will give you leave to preach against their sins as much as you will, and talk as much for godliness in the pulpit, so you will but let them alone afterwards, and be friendly and merry with them when you have done, and talk as they do, and live as they, and be indifferent with them in your conference and conversation. For they take the pulpit to be but as a stage; a place where preachers must show themselves and play their parts, where you have liberty to say what you list for an hour . . . (1950: 168)

Sometimes we need to urge people to do, or not to do, something, but the normal mood of Christian preaching should be indicative, not imperative. (The indicative mood describes a fact, e.g. 'God loved the world'; the imperative describes a command, e.g. 'love one another'.) In other words, like Paul, we should spend most of our time reminding people of what God has done for them in the past, is doing in them now and will do for them in the future. When we do this, it is 'good news' and we are on sure ground; when we tell them *how* to live, we probably do not know enough about their lives to give them good advice. Most of the work of application to life can be left to the inward work of the Holy Spirit. At times, however, we may enlist the help of others. A young woman who had just been ordained was told to preach on 'Honesty in Business'. She had no experience at all of business practice, but was able to preach effectively by asking a businessman in her congregation to help her by giving his testimony. We need to use all the resources God has given us – both human beings and his Holy Spirit.

Add/Subtract

Now return to your notes and imagine that you are listening to them for the first time. You will probably have much more material than you can use in one sermon. But first, before you take anything out, check the main sections of your sermon. You may have anything from two to six of these; but more important than how many you have is how clear is the connection between them. You need to make the connections crystal clear, so that the hearers can see the logic of your argument. If a connection is not clear, add material to clarify it. If you find this to be impossible, you will probably need to cut out one of the sections altogether.

Second, ask 'What difficult words have I used or difficult problems have I raised?' Either *add* the necessary explanation or *subtract* the problem. Language can also be a problem, especially for those who have been trained in theology. They may need to do some hard work on this. C. S. Lewis wrote, 'Let us use language which is simple and memorable; any fool can make things difficult', and 'Turn your faith into ordinary language; if you cannot do so, either you don't understand it, or you don't believe it.' One way of ensuring that we understand what we are talking about is to try to say it in your second or third language. Using a language different from one's mother tongue is a discipline which makes us ask what we really do mean! *Subtract* therefore all jargon, dull passages and repetitions of words and phrases.

Third, are your hearers likely to feel better, or worse, after your sermon? Too much challenge or too much idealism can be very depressing, unless you give a lot of encouragement in the way that Jesus invariably did to those who felt inadequate. It was never the 'sinners' whom Jesus criticized, but those who were religious and self-satisfied. He always showed sinners a way out and helped them to feel better about themselves (see Luke 19.1–10). A useful exercise is to ask yourself, 'What does it feel like to be a 14-year-old boy, or a pregnant teenager, or a university professor, or a mother who is HIV-positive, or a homeless refugee, or a prosperous businessman – and how will such a person respond to this sermon?'

Remember, too, that in most churches there are some who don't care – they are only there because that is their habit on Sundays. Aim to show them their need. Others don't know – aim to teach them what God's word says. Others don't believe – try to give them examples of how God is at work in the lives of real people.

Finally, *subtract* anything that does not serve your aim, however important in itself it may be. Be ruthless – after all, this is not your last sermon, so you can always use the extra material some other time.

Style

Use plenty of short sentences. Include phrases which are not full sentences, such as exclamations, questions, etc. Use the colloquial, everyday language you hear on the street, which would probably not look correct if written down. That is what writers in the New Testament did – they would not have won many prizes in Greek language tests! Use concrete nouns and verbs which people can 'see' rather than abstract ideas; active verbs rather than passive ones. Avoid flowery language, which is more likely to impress people than to change them. Alter the tone and speed of your delivery (fast for something dramatic, slow and even repetitive, for emphasis). When reciting a quotation or poem, show that you are reading it from a book or paper. If you are reporting what someone said or thought, quote their direct speech (i.e. the actual words they said). Use pauses; mix humour with solemnity; mix light with shadow. Don't either stand like a statue or walk around constantly, but use moderate gestures. But at the end, ask yourself whether you want people to congratulate you on your excellent sermon, or whether you want them to hear the voice of God and be changed. People are often changed when preachers are at their worst, not at their best; and you will be surprised! See p. 32.

The Writing

Some experienced preachers write out their sermons word for word. It is good for everyone to try out this practice at some time in their training. But it is not the best method for everyone to use, for it is easy for the written word to become a barrier between the preacher and the listeners. Also the way most people write is not the best way to speak. At the other extreme, one Pakistani bishop goes into the pulpit with nothing written at all. It is all in his head, and he speaks with never a note and never a hesitation. He has prepared well, but not on paper.

Everyone will have their own method. I once saw the late Bishop Festo Kivengere go to preach with just a few ideas scribbled on the back of an envelope. He preached on these for 20 minutes, then abandoned his 'notes' for the last 20 minutes – everyone was spellbound and deeply moved.

Festo was once preparing for preaching together with a European colleague in a mission in Nairobi. The European sat with Bible, commentaries and a large notepad, working out a neat three-point address, but found he was distracted by seeing Festo sitting relaxed with an open Bible, just meditating, praying and occasionally jotting down an idea. Both of them spent hours in preparation; they just did it differently (Coomes, 1990:290). Do not follow Festo's example until you have had years of practice! But notice also that these two men were typical of the cultures they came from. Those who come from a culture built around conversation and relationships find it easy to speak spontaneously. Those whose culture and education is built on books and private reflection usually need help from written notes or text.

Colin Morris (1996:95) describes four methods. First, write down every word; then read it. Second, write it, leave it at home and recite it from memory. He calls these 'the two worst methods'. Third, write it out, master it and then speak from summary notes. Fourth, Morris' own method is to work out the structure fully in his mind, then speak it, trusting that the appropriate words will come to him. There is actually a fifth method, specially designed for lazy preachers – don't prepare at all, but trust the Holy Spirit to give you the right words.

My own method is similar to Morris' third. I write my thoughts and structure on paper, and then write my notes on 6 × 4 inch (152 × 102 mm) index cards, for four reasons:

1 They are stiff card and do not flutter about.
2 They fit neatly between the pages of my Bible, which is useful in the open air or when there is no place for notes.
3 They easily slot into my sermon filing system.
4 They are big enough to contain the skeleton of my sermon.

Nowadays I use only one side of one card; but when I began to preach I used to fill three or four sides! But for the end result to be worthwhile, you must be ready to take risks and feel free to say things you have never prepared but which God brings into your mind. Whatever your method, try to sound warm and personal, and maintain eye-contact with the congregation. Pick out two or three people who are sitting in different parts of the church, and look at them.

On rare occasions you may have to alter your whole sermon at the last minute because of some totally unexpected happening (examples are given on pp. 5–6), or even because you feel inwardly convinced that God wants you to bring the congregation a different message. In this case, tell the congregation what you are doing and why – then they will certainly give you their support and their attention.

File your sermons according to the book and chapter of your text. It is then easy to find them again for future use. Also write upon them when and where they were preached. But note the words quoted by John Wesley, on p. 78!

The Opening

If any part of the sermon is more important than any other, then this is it! This is where you must 'register' with the congregation. This is where they will decide whether to pay attention or go to sleep. This is where you must arouse their interest. Some preachers do this by telling a joke. This is disastrous, unless the joke is going to be effectively used to connect with some serious point in the sermon. If it does not, a joke is telling the congregation that you are aiming to entertain them but not to make a serious contribution to their faith and life. I am assuming that before you begin you will have silently asked God to help you, then prayed out loud that he will speak to everyone present – and at this time a moment or two of silence might be appropriate.

If, however, you are a visiting preacher, you must first of all spend a few moments introducing yourself, thanking them for their welcome, bringing greetings from the community you belong to and perhaps establishing a personal link between you and the congregation.

Never apologize for yourself or your sermon (except in the case involving unexpected events mentioned above). You may feel ill, you may have forgotten your notes, you may be preaching your first sermon ever, you may have good reason to be utterly depressed and sad – but the congregation have got quite enough problems of their own without being saddled with yours as well. They will not understand your problems of sermon preparation, and you cannot expect their sympathy.

Never make an extravagant claim for your message, such as 'This is the most significant verse in the whole Bible.' It will not hold their attention because they just won't believe you.

Never begin your sermon by stating what is obvious or what is just boring. A preacher entered the pulpit to preach at the Harvest Festival just after the harvest hymns had been sung. He was surrounded by green leaves, fruit, flowers, maize cobs and cucumbers. Looking like a bird in a nest, he solemnly began, 'Today is our Harvest Festival.' Another preacher took a text from Jeremiah, and began, 'Jeremiah was a prophet who lived in the second century before Christ. He preached in Judah, the southern kingdom, and his ministry spanned five reigns over a period of 40 years. You can read about his times in 2 Kings 22–5.' By this time everyone had stopped listening. He would have done better to begin, 'The man we are thinking about this morning would have annoyed many of you. He mixed religion with politics.' By now everybody would be sitting up, eager to hear more (Manson, 1984:60).

Openings register with the listeners when they mention a matter of topical interest, or tell an interesting story, or show that the sermon will deal with a matter of vital relevance to faith and life, or say something entirely unexpected. Jesus caught people's attention by all four methods. A good general rule is to focus on your listeners at the start and end of the sermon, but on the text in the middle of it. Even though the Bible text is the most important part of the sermon, it is not always necessary to announce it at the start. Sometimes it may come after the introductory remarks. On occasions it may even come at the end, as in Paul's sermon in Acts 20.35.

The Old Testament scholar, Walter Brueggemann, warned a class of theological students,

> The pastors of the church must make an outrageous act of subversive rationality. You cannot conduct ministry on the basis of the rationality of our culture, because if you do, there isn't any good news. I do not know what you are taught about preaching, but the place where I notice it is in long sermon introductions. Long sermon introductions are basically designed to assure the congregation that 'I'm not going to say anything that does not fit in with everything that you've already thought'. One of the things about Karl Barth's sermons is they don't have any introductions. He just starts: and the very first sentence he utters calls the whole world into question. (Brueggemann, 1987)

Another scholar put it like this:

> We must reach out to the culture if we are to preach the gospel. On the other hand we are to distinguish ourselves from the culture to display the sign of God's new age. One impulse is world-relating; the other world-rejecting. (Buttrick, 1994:75)

Preachers must have the courage to do this and offer the people a completely new way of looking at life (see p. 106), just as Jesus did, and most of the writers in the Bible. If we do not do so, 'There isn't any good news.'

The Ending

It is essential to write out your last paragraph in full, even though you may not finalize it until just before the service begins – because one of the biggest problems facing inexperienced preachers is how to bring their sermon to an end. They feel like a plane looking for a suitable place to land, while the sermon gets longer and longer in the process! You need to be flexible about it until the last minute, because the situation may alter in a way that makes you alter the way you end. In this way you will identify with the response which the people make to God's word at that particular time and in that particular place. Quite often the preacher will want to write a final paragraph which emphasizes the aim. But the best way to do that may not be simply to restate your aim. It will probably be more effective to finish with a memorable text (like Acts 20.35), or to tie the end in with the way you began (Mark 4.9), or to refer back briefly to a specially memorable story or illustration you used earlier (Luke 15.32), or even to tell a new story which suggests a proper response to that message. You might decide to leave the congregation with a question for them to ponder and answer in the form of a response in their lives (Luke 10.36), or to leave them with a pointed challenge to their usual way of thinking (Acts 2.36). Endings like this recognize that the true ending of any sermon lies not in the preacher's words but in the attitudes and actions of preacher and people alike. Such endings leave people in suspense – they do not tell them what to do, but leave them to 'see' and respond for themselves (see p. 115).

Do not have several conclusions – choose just one. Do not introduce any new ideas into your ending (though a new illustration is allowable). Don't say 'finally . . .' until you really mean it!

Probably the reason why Jesus told so many parables to the crowds was in order 'to accommodate Himself to their capacity and . . . keep the attention of the hearers awake till a more convenient time, allowing them to remain in a state of suspense' (Calvin, quoted in Cranfield, 1977:171). Cranfield goes on,

> Had he spoken to them in a direct way, he would have forced them to make a final decision at once, and that decision could only have been a decision of unbelief and rejection. Instead he spoke to them in an indirect way, thus engaging and maintaining their interest, and summoning them to decision without compelling them to make a final decision immediately. The parabolic teaching was at once a judgment pronounced upon their unpreparedness for the kingdom of God and also the expression of divine mercy that desires to spare and to save.

Jesus made them think for themselves about what his words really meant, and weigh up the arguments for and against becoming his disciples. See also John 6.60, 66–8; Mark 4.9, 10, 13.

After finishing your preparation, you should ask yourself three questions, as follows:

1 Have I addressed their minds, their feelings and their wills? In Romans 6.17, Paul showed that he believed that the gospel was *reasonable*, i.e. it was 'teaching' which appealed to people's powers of reason. He also believed that it was *emotional*, i.e. it affected their 'hearts' or feelings, making them upset or joyful (see Acts 2.37). Finally, he believed that it was *transforming*, i.e. it affected their wills, making them 'obedient' to its demands (see Acts 2.41, 42). The message of God provides us with a basis for action, a motive for action and a proper course of action. Christians in Base Christian Communities in Latin America, when they meet to study the Bible, often finish up by asking, '*Who* will do *what* and *when*?' (Bowen, 1996:183).

2 Have I spoken about Jesus? (See p. 23) He is the subject of the New Testament and the fulfilment of the Old. Festo Kivengere was once asked to go to minister to three men who were about to be executed by order of the Ugandan dictator, Idi Amin. 'What on earth can I say which will make sense to these young men?' he asked himself, and felt Jesus answering him, 'Tell them about me, and I will make sense.'

3 Finally, after preparing and before preaching, ask yourself if there is any part of your sermon about which you feel uncertain. Outside help is invaluable, so get advice from a friend or, best of all, your wife or husband. You could even rehearse your sermon with them, or record it on tape and listen to that. And when you come to preach, get a friend to tell you if you are speaking too softly or too loudly, especially if an electronic microphone is being used. If you are inexperienced, the same friend could help you, by means of a signal, to know when it is time to stop.

Afterwards

What should follow your sermon? There can be no one answer to this question. The old East African United Liturgy recognized this by allowing freedom for a variety of responses. Sometimes it will be appropriate for the congregation to stand and together confess their faith in God. It may be more suitable to respond by praying for those in need, or by confessing our sins, or simply by waiting in complete silence for God to speak to us individually. Very often the best response is to sing a suitable hymn, perhaps of praise, and it will not be surprising if the preached word leads most naturally into sharing bread and wine together in the Eucharist, just as it probably did when 1 Corinthians was read aloud to its first recipients.

You may hope that people will praise your sermon afterwards, but it is more important that they should praise Christ and respond as he wants them to. However, we must face the fact that 'The Sermon is Me', whether we like it or not. People who know you well will always take more notice of who you are than of how well you speak! Often 'it is not the sermons that people dislike; it is the personality through whom such sermons come' (Kurewa, 2000:173). 'The aim of preparation is clear; it is a man prepared, not a sermon prepared' (Knox, 1957:76). 'Be yourself,' was Kivengere's advice. 'Don't be like Jacob pretending to be Esau to get the blessing. You must be willing to take the skins off and be you' (Coomes, 1990:216).

At such times, when you are bound to feel self-conscious and uncertain how to respond when people praise you, criticize you or (worst of all) ignore you, it is good to remember that God will speak to people more through your doubts than through your confidence, more through your weaknesses than through your strengths, more through your suffering than through your success, more through your questions than through your answers. It is clear that Jesus made the greatest impression on his disciples when he girded himself with a towel and washed their feet, and when he hung, apparently helplessly, on the cross. We distance ourselves from people when we display great competence as preachers, but if we can share their sorrows and perplexities, then we show we understand where they are, and can invite them to come with us to a better place.

Preachers very soon learn that there is no connection between the apparent excellence of sermons and the effect they have on the hearers. At times someone will thank you for a sermon which you did not preach but which they heard. In other words, God spoke not because of you, but in spite of you! Paul found long ago that the way God builds his kingdom does not follow the normal rules of human success and failure. He saved the world through a man who died rejected, powerless and apparently defeated. It is good if preachers recognize this at a very early stage. To do so will protect them both from pride and from discouragement.

Barbara Brown Taylor helps us to understand this by relating her experience that a sermon she had carefully prepared proved to be a bad one, but a sermon at a baby's funeral which she had not prepared, because she was overcome by grief, was good. Someone transcribed it, and when she read it afterwards, she made the following comments (Taylor, 1993:85):

> It was nothing but a jumble of phrases and images, trailing off into awkward silence. While the Holy Spirit was in them . . . they lived. Afterwards they were no more than empty boxes lying where the wind had blown them. These two experiences remind me not to take myself too

seriously. They also make me reluctant to talk about 'best' and 'worst' sermons. Something happens between the preacher's lips and the congregation that is beyond prediction or explanation. The same sermon sounds entirely different at 9 and at 11.15 on Sunday morning. Sermons that make me weep leave my listeners baffled, and sermons that seem cold to me find warm response.

The gospel is not complicated but simple. Many people expressed surprise that Billy Graham's sermons actually had the same content as everyone else's; his power came from an anointing of the Holy Spirit. His message to Cambridge University students was basically the same as his message to a bunch of drunks in an African village (Coomes, 1990:202) – but no doubt expressed in different forms.

How long does it take to prepare a sermon? One famous preacher said that every five minutes of preaching requires one hour of preparation. However, this takes no account of the fact that no preacher just 'writes' a sermon: on the contrary, preachers live their sermons for days and days before they preach them – or at least they should do so. And not just days – years, for the Bible must become the air you breathe if you are to preach it. You cannot switch on and off at will a message that you believe God is giving you to bring (see Jeremiah 20.9). If you can, you have no right to stand with God's word on your lips. So preparation time will, ideally, be no less than a week – but in that time you may have to work on not just one, but three or four sermons!

The shorter the sermon, the longer it may take to prepare. A four-minute talk for a TV *Epilogue* or a radio *Thought for the Day* is likely to take far longer than your half-hour Sunday sermon. But preachers who are honest will often admit that, with careful preparation, they can sometimes say as much in four minutes as they do in their usual 30-minute sermon which is less carefully prepared. The French philosopher, Blaise Pascal, in 1657 apologized to a friend of his: 'I am sorry to have written such a long letter, but I have not had the time to make it shorter' (1920:210).

Special Note A
USING THE LECTIONARY

Lectionaries (sometimes called church calendars) are of several different types. Some churches do not use lectionaries at all in their services, in which case preachers preach on a topic, passage or verse of their choice, or follow the church's 'teaching programme' (see p. 4).

But Roman Catholics, Anglicans, Lutherans and many others follow a lectionary. This is a sequence of Bible readings organized in a cycle of one, two or three years. The aim is first to cover the main events of the Christian year, and second to provide a balanced diet of teaching for regular worshippers. In such situations, preachers should normally follow that particular lectionary, which may include passages from the Old Testament, Psalms, New Testament Epistles (with Acts and Revelation) and Gospels – and even a special prayer (or collect) which reflects the theme. There are different patterns of lectionaries, as follows:

1 *Thematic*: Every Sunday has a theme, probably determined by the main reading, often but not always the Gospel. Other readings fit in with that key reading or theme.
2 *Continuous*: There is a continuity in the readings (or at least in some of them) from Sunday to Sunday, especially during Advent, Epiphany, Lent or after Pentecost. This aims to give the congregation regular teaching on the message of a particular book or writer.
3 *Ecclesiastical*: The above patterns are often combined with certain seasons, or Sundays, especially around Christmas, Easter and Pentecost, when all the readings focus on the events being celebrated at that time.

Preachers need to use the lectionary wisely. At the great festivals of the Church the sermon should focus on the great events being commemorated. At other times a custom has grown up of attempting to preach a sermon which mentions *all* the readings set in the lectionary, sometimes even trying to include the psalm and collect as well. This is difficult to do, and should not be encouraged, because it creates a new 'context' for the sermon which comes not from the biblical writer but from the people who compiled the church lectionary. If preachers are servants of the word of God in Scripture, they should take their text seriously in the setting it had when it was first written. That is the only way to show people that the Bible must speak for itself and sit in judgement on the church which hears it. People do not want to hear ideas which come just from the preacher or the compilers of the lectionary.

The lectionary is a good servant but a bad master.

1 It helps preachers to choose their topic to fit in with the church's journey through the year.
2 It covers all the parts of the Bible, even those which the preacher might not personally choose.
3 Therefore, it stops preachers from becoming dry or repetitive.
4 It gives the congregation a sense of being on the same journey not only with their own fellowship but also with their sister congregations (Kurewa, 2000:162).

On the other hand, because of the needs of the people or the events of the previous week, preachers will often be led by the Holy Spirit to depart from the set readings and to preach on something else – and in that case the wise pastor will be willing to alter the set readings accordingly.

Study Suggestions

1 What were the aims of (a) Luke and (b) John in writing their Gospels, and (c) of John in writing his first Epistle? What effects would they have hoped to see in their readers' lives?
2 In what ways did a sermon you recently heard (or preached) lead people to (a) feel, (b) believe and (c) do anything? Was any one of these three dimensions lacking?
3 What was the real purpose of the writers of (a) Isaiah 5.1–7; (b) Amos 1—2; (c) Romans 2?
4 Read Ephesians 4.7–16. What is this text trying to do? What information does it give? What needs of the readers is it trying to address? What needs, if any, in your own church could it meet? Outline a sermon on this text, using language and ideas of today.
5 In your opinion, what are the advantages and disadvantages of:

(a) preaching from a full script?
(b) preaching from notes?
(c) memorizing your sermon?

6 Give examples of Jesus' four methods (p. 29) of catching people's attention.
7 How does the Old Testament sermon outlined on p. 126 speak of Jesus? How far do you agree with the statement that every sermon should direct people's thoughts to Jesus?

8 Why did the parables in Matthew 20.1–16 and Luke 18.9–14 shock or challenge those who first heard them? In what ways, if any, might they challenge listeners today?

9 What do you find surprising when you read Mark 1.40–5? Note especially 'anger' (NRSV marg.), 'touched', 'sent away', 'testimony'.

10 Ask three preachers how long they take to prepare their sermons and ask three church members how long they like sermons to be. What guidance do you get from their answers?

11 What Bible reading (lectionary) system does your church follow? How helpful do people find it, and what are its strengths and weaknesses?

3

WHAT IS PREACHING?

[At the inn on Sunday after the service] they invariably discussed the sermon, dissecting it, weighing it, as above or below the average – the general tendency being to regard it as a scientific feat or performance which had no relation to their own lives, except as between critics and the thing criticized.

Thomas Hardy, *The Mayor of Casterbridge*, ch. 33, 1886

Some Traditional Views

'It pleased God by the foolishness of preaching to save them that believe' (1 Corinthians 1.21 KJV).
'Christianity stands or falls with preaching; it is God's act of redemption' – P. T. Forsyth.
'It is God's answer to the people's question' – Karl Barth.
'Preaching is truth through personality' – Phillips Brooks.
'Only in preaching can the salvation-occurrence happen' – R. Bultmann.
'Preaching is converting life into truth' – Ralph Waldo Emerson.
'The preacher stands between the soul and God; there eternal destinies are determined' – Martyn Lloyd-Jones.
'John Wesley alone (by preaching) prevented England from sliding into a bloody revolution.'

These quotations come from the Western world 50 years ago or more. Famous preachers could expect to proclaim an authoritative message to large crowds in church or in the open air and change their lives. But there were others who held a different view.

The Value of Preaching Questioned

The English novelist Anthony Trollope wrote: 'There is, perhaps, no greater hardship inflicted on mankind in civilized and free countries than the necessity of listening to sermons.' Trollope was trying to be humorous but today most people in Europe would agree with him.

Gerhard Ebeling complained that most modern preaching was just an incomprehensible 'recitation of the traditional word of God' and quoted

Dietrich Bonhoeffer, writing a year before his execution by Hitler in Nazi Germany in 1945:

> The Church is incapable of being the bearer of the reconciling and saving word . . . that is why the old words fail and fall silent, and our Christian life consists only of prayer and of doing the right things among men . . . It is not for us to foretell the day, but the day will come when men will be called to utter the Word of God in such a way that the world is changed and renewed. There will be a new language, perhaps quite unreligious but liberating and saving, like the language of Jesus, so that men are horrified at it and yet conquered by its power . . . which tells of the peace of God and the coming of His Kingdom. (1961:184)

That was written over 60 years ago, but today the Church in the Western world is hearing such opinions again. David Norrington has recently claimed that traditional forms of preaching in our churches tend to produce immature Christians who learn to be dependent on the professional clergy. It was not like that in New Testament times, he writes, when preachers could be challenged and even contradicted. He wants the church to rediscover the cell-church pattern when people met together in local groups, exercised their different gifts and involved everyone in ministry. The one-person sermon to a silent congregation should be a thing of the past (Norrington, 1996).

When I was planning to write this Guide, a mission leader in London said to me, 'On preaching? That's a bit out of date, isn't it?' The normal length of a sermon in the Church of England is now seven to twelve minutes. Even then, people often find it boring and irrelevant, and want it to be even shorter. This is because modern life has changed in four chief ways:

1 *Authority*: People question whether anyone has the authority to tell them what to believe or how to behave. Even radio and TV invite listeners to give their opinions on a par with the 'experts', so pastors should not pretend to be experts in anything. Any suggestion of dominance, control and authority will be resisted in most modern cultures. People respect pastors who are real and authentic and who know what it is to fail, to suffer and to doubt. It is better to weep with those who weep than to give neat answers. The ideal is that God should make his word incarnate – in the person of a preacher who has met with God, and is authentic because of it.

2 *Education*: Most people have some education and skills. While 200 years ago the pastor was probably the best-educated person in the district, this is no longer the case. People know there are two or more sides to every question. Many are better educated than the

pastor. They may feel the Church's message is predictable and unlikely to contain anything new – just the traditional teaching and moralizing. The issues facing people today are complex – so we need a debate which will use everyone's gifts, not reflect just one person's point of view. The congregations in the Church of the New Testament seem to have been like this. They had not one leader but many. They told their stories and shared good and bad experiences. They responded and asked questions. Today lay people have experiences of life which the preacher cannot have, so their insights and wisdom are needed. Let us not control them, but release them.

3 *Entertainment*: The cinema, radio and TV provide people with professional entertainment, even in their homes. By comparison, people will find preachers unskilled and tedious. They will stay at home rather than come to church. Even Christians may find services on TV or radio more inspiring than those in their own church. Preachers are not primarily in the business of entertaining, but Augustine thought that one of the aims of a preacher should be 'to delight' the hearers. (The other two aims, he said, are to teach and to influence.) Preachers must 'take pleasure and delight in what they are saying – if so, they will be heard with pleasure, for so great is the power of sympathy.'

4 *Communication*: Before the invention of writing, people communicated just by talking. Perhaps a group, sitting round the fire, would use stories, songs and things they could see or smell. Marshall McLuhan, writing in the 1960s, called this sort of communication 'cool'. (This is a technical term used in communication theory.) People use all their senses as they take part, but do not have to concentrate much. The invention of writing – and even more, of printing in 1450 – invited people to use their eyes and brains and absorb new information sitting down in a quiet corner with just a book. McLuhan called this 'hot' communication. There was plenty of information on the page, which did not require much work from the reader apart from receiving the message. It was a private, individual activity. Readers began to 'see' words in their minds not only when they were reading, but even when they were conversing with other people. They lost the power of memory and of spontaneous improvisation. They felt free to separate from their family and clan, because they no longer depended on others. They stopped saying, 'We are; therefore I am' and began to say, 'I think; therefore I am.' This has become characteristic of people who live in the global North. They have less time for relationships and often seem to be in a hurry. People of the South seem to them to be often 'late' or 'inefficient'. This is not so; it is just that their cultural priorities are quite different.

Long ago Plato showed that writing had its disadvantages. In his book *Phaedrus*, someone claimed that the discovery of writing made the Egyptians wiser and improved their memories.

> 'No,' replied Socrates, 'it will plant forgetfulness in their souls; they will cease to exercise memory because they rely on that which is written, calling things to remembrance no longer from within themselves, but by means of external marks . . . and it is no true wisdom that you offer, but only its appearance; for by telling them of many things without teaching them you will make them seem to know much, while for the most part they know nothing'. (Plato, 1972:275A)

Those who still live within an oral culture hear and speak many more words than they ever read, have retained the power of memory and, because they do not rely on words they see on a page, are skilled at improvising in drama, poetry and public speaking. This is the culture in which the epic poem (Greek, Arabic, Swahili, etc.) developed, and so did West Indian calypso-singing. The precise words are not known until the speaker stands up and begins. The words of the poem or drama vary from performance to performance – whereas people brought up in a reading culture stop to correct themselves if they 'get the words wrong'. In general, therefore, those who belong to the cultural South (sometimes called 'the developing world' or 'the Third World') find it much easier to preach without notes or manuscript than those whose thinking is controlled by the written word. They also get emotionally involved, and involve their hearers, using repetitions and standard forms of expression which make the audience join in. For them words are not 'things', but powerful actions which create relationships. In most parts of Africa, market traders seem to want chiefly to interact with their customers in the bargaining game. Whether the customer buys the goods or not seems to matter less than the enjoyment which the people, including the bystanders, get out of the game. That is how preaching is done in the South. It is really enjoyable!

The medium of television is having the effect of gradually bringing people of the North (i.e. the 'Western' world) back to an oral culture. This means that preachers have to modify their method and use, as Jesus did, more short sound bites, images and stories which stir the imagination, instead of closely argued, deductive reasoning leading to certain clear conclusions. Relating, interacting and participating are now the basic essentials in every culture. This is an area in which the North has much to learn from the South. Those preachers who have been educated in traditional Western university methods will often spend much time preparing their words and arguments, to perfect an error-free presentation but, to use McLuhan's terminology, if we are preaching 'hot' and the people are thinking 'cool', they will just walk away.

Biblical Words for Preaching

The two most common words for preaching in the New Testament are *kerusso* and *euangelizomai*, from which we get the English words 'kerygmatic' and 'evangelize'. These refer to bringing a new message (*kerygma*) or proclaiming the good news (*euangelion*) of what God has done – often to people who have not heard it before. Paul summarized this message in 1 Corinthians 15.3–11, where he also used the word *paradosis*, which means the tradition handed down from Christ and then passed on to others. It reminds preachers that they must be faithful to the message they have received. The tradition does not consist only of the Gospel. It also includes Christian teaching about doctrine (*didache*) or behaviour (sometimes called *paraineseis* or, more often, *parangelia*). Writers in the New Testament often said they were just 'reminding' their readers of things which they knew already. 'People more frequently need to be reminded than informed', said Dr Samuel Johnson.

A study of the above words shows us that it is not the *activity* of preaching which has power, but the message preached, i.e. the *kerygma*. The message can reach people not only by preaching but by books, drama, art, song, behaviour, etc. That is what the Greek of 1 Corinthians 1.21 actually says: 'It pleased God by the foolishness of the *kerygma* to save those who believe' – contrast the KJV translation quoted on p. 37.

However, the most fundamental means of communication is person to person. In the view of Colin Morris, 'Every form of communication of the gospel other than eyeball to eyeball contact is in some way defective' (Morris, 1995). That is how God communicated with us in Jesus, and in doing so revealed not just a message (as Muslims believe) but himself in person. Most of the writings in the New Testament were primarily not words on paper, but words spoken, then written down and finally read out loud to the listeners. See p. 101.

Some Definitions for Today

There are very many ways of defining or describing preaching. Readers should think up their own definitions. Those which follow contain a lot of wisdom and can give us some ideas.

1 A good sermon is one rooted in the Bible interpreted for the twentieth century, finding its ratification [confirming support] in the tradition and experience of the Church and in the preacher's own experience,

evoking the kind of Christian faith that has an easy relevance to the daily lives of its hearers. (Stacey, 1980:22)

2 Preaching involves both a message and a medium. It must be *verbal*, for God's acts are interpreted acts, and *personal*, for God has revealed himself personally and makes present here and now the redemption which is in Christ.

3 A sermon should bring together four aspects of the word of God:

   (a) the living word, Christ, who should in some way be the focus of every sermon;
   (b) the written word, Scripture, which the preacher must expound and disclose;
   (c) the spoken word, which relates personally to the hearers through the preacher;
   (d) the symbolic word, the Church, in which 'the mission of Jesus continues not only as proclamation of the kingdom, but also as the presence of the kingdom in the form of death and resurrection'. (Lesslie Newbigin, adapted)

4 Preaching is an encounter of the Word of God in Scripture with the people in their concrete, historical situation, so that the living word of God always occurs at the point of intersection of the message of the text with the situation. The minister acts in solidarity with his congregation – how, he does not know beforehand – he has to reflect on both the text and the congregation. (Runia, 1983:36, 65)

5 Biblical preaching is the proclamation of the gospel to people in relation to their contemporary life, through faithful exposition of the Scriptures, as one is empowered by the Holy Spirit. Such proclamation often concludes with an invitation for a decision or action. (Kurewa, 2000:92)

6 To preach is to open up the inspired text with such faithfulness to the text and such sensitivity to the modern context that God's voice is heard and His people obey Him. (John Stott)

7 Preaching is the organized hallelujah of the ordered congregation. (P. T. Forsyth)

The Role of the Congregation

It is easy for Christian ministers to think that preaching a sermon is a performance. They are responsible for preaching a good sermon, and the people listen and may decide whether it is good or bad. But the definitions above show that the listeners have an important part to play in the preaching of every sermon. The way Paul spoke at Athens was determined by what he saw and what he heard from the philosophers to whom he spoke. When he wrote to the Colossians, he used the sort of language which they used themselves. In his letter to the Romans, he was always asking, 'How are they reacting to my words?' and then answering their unspoken questions. Karl Barth said that the preacher should have the Bible in one hand and the daily newspaper in the other. Today we might add '. . . and have the TV on in the background'. Here are some ways in which the listeners are involved in the sermon:

1 The Bible is *their* book, not the preacher's only. Earlier members of the Church wrote down the canonical Scriptures, and then recognized them as the God-given word under which the people were to sit. In the Bible, God is talking not to the ignorant but to those who are made in his image and understand his language. The people of God *are* the experts. It is their tradition and they have the authority to interpret it. Hence Paul repeatedly asks his readers, 'Do you not know . . . ?' In response to preaching, the listeners have the freedom to say 'Yes' or 'No'. When Augustine preached about 'peace in our borders', his hearers responded with loud acclamations – it was this for which they were longing, and he knew it. But sometimes they want to say, 'It does not seem like that to me', and preachers should encourage this. We want Christians to think for themselves, and raise the questions and problems which they feel. If new light is to come to us from the Scriptures, the Holy Spirit will probably bring it to us through the people in whom he lives and works. If we silence them, we may be silencing him!

2 Preachers should relate their sermons to the situation, experiences, thoughts, problems and questions of the congregation. One good way of doing that is by visiting the people regularly in their homes – not to speak, but to listen, and to understand some of the problems they are facing. But it is important to be sensitive. A sermon on family life must never forget people who have no happy family for one reason or another (see p. 17). People are uplifted and encouraged after listening to someone who understands how they feel. But too often the Church answers questions no one is asking – and that just makes people depressed. It is more important to show understanding than to produce answers. People will always listen to a preacher who can describe how they are feeling in a certain situation, and often there are no real answers except those which people find by experience.

Some of the world's greatest writers did this effectively. One good example is the Russian novelist, Fyodor Dostoevsky. In his book *The Brothers Karamazov*, he described the suffering of children in poor families. Ivan Karamazov is very angry at the way these children are abused. He is angry not only with those who abuse them, but also with God. 'Why,' he asks, 'does God allow these terrible things to happen?' In our world today, many people ask the same question. Ivan's brother, Alyosha, answers that in the world to come God will put right all these evil abuses. But Ivan is not satisfied. Dostoevsky never answers the problem – but he completely understands how people feel and why they are angry with God. Indeed, he shares their anger. This is called 'empathy', and preachers need to understand and to empathize with those who suffer. In the same way, the writer of the book of Job understands exactly how Job feels, even though he can give no easy answers.

Another writer who was skilled at understanding pain and suffering is Shusaku Endo, of Japan. In his book *Silence*, and in other novels, he describes the suffering of Japanese Christians during the state persecution in the seventeenth century, and he relates their pain to the suffering love of Jesus. Jesus knows what it is to suffer for and with his people. He himself is angry at injustice in the world (see p. 97). Like Jesus, Endo empathizes with those who suffer, and preachers must do the same, 'weeping with those who weep' (see Romans 12.15). Chapter 8 shows how Siméa Meldrum did this in Brazil. The plight of the poor people on the rubbish tip made her angry – and eventually enabled her to understand them and to preach to them and for them.

3 Sermons should reflect the wisdom of the congregation. God is always enriching his Church through people who come from other cultures or other situations. Abbot Franzoni in Rome spent a couple of hours one Saturday with 150 disabled people. They all used their Bibles to help him prepare the sermon for the following day, so the sermon was not his but theirs. We should acknowledge the ideas we get from other people by saying, 'As Mrs D'Souza was telling me yesterday . . .' or, 'Brother Njoroge told me the story of how the church first came to this village . . .' Then everyone realizes that they all have a part to play. The choir or music group play their part by singing or leading songs which reinforce the message. They are part of the preacher's team, and they should consult together for their joint ministry. We preachers do not come *to* the congregation, we come *from* it (Morris, 1996:120).

4 Sermons should challenge the way people think, not by 'scolding' them for faults or wrong attitudes, but by reminding them that the worldly or secular way of interpreting events or actions, which we see on TV or read in our newspapers, is completely different from the way we should understand the world through the eyes of faith. In the days of apartheid, the Church in South Africa offered an

integrationist model of thought and behaviour for which people longed. It was completely different from the daily life they were forced to live. So, too, the prophets of the Jewish Scriptures and the apostles, like Jesus, were prepared to 'call the whole world into question' (see p. 29).

5 The people should be expected to react to preaching. Martin Luther King Jr's hearers did this by clapping or calling out 'Amen', 'Hallelujah', 'Preach it', 'Yes, sir', 'Make it plain'. A sermon should never be a monologue, but always a dialogue. Preachers must open up a conversation between the people and the God who is being proclaimed, just as people get involved when watching an interesting TV programme together (see p. 14). Dialogue, whether spoken or silent, helps people to continue to reflect on their faith together and on their own throughout the week.

6 When listening to God's message relating to their situation, people may expect to be touched by the Spirit of God and be changed. Preaching is the God above speaking to the God within, and Christians ought to pray for the preacher before and during the sermon. Even non-Christians have the witness of God within them from what he reveals to them in creation around or in conscience within. So they too can be expected to respond to what he reveals through his spoken word.

7 Preachers sometimes speak *for* the people, not just to them. The preacher is the people's voice. After the Second World War, Winston Churchill, the British Prime Minister, said, 'The British people were the lion; it just fell to me to give the roar.' In the same way the preacher's task is to discern the mood of the people and express how they feel and to say what they know to be true – because they cannot say it for themselves. This often happens, but especially at funerals and other times of crisis or pain. See p. 73.

8 The people should have the opportunity of responding to the sermon and speaking back to the preacher and to one another. If they have been stimulated to think about God and about their lives, then they should share those thoughts with others. Sometimes this will happen within a family as they talk afterwards; at other times it will be possible to arrange a group discussion after the service.

9 If preaching is to be effective, then this is not the business of the preacher only. The congregation, as the main support group, should somehow be informed about what God is doing. This will encourage them to get further involved, especially in praying for the preaching in the church.

This can only happen if our preaching has an element of interactive participation about it. Space should be made for members of the congregation to bear *witness* to what God is doing in their lives. The element of personal experience was fundamental to the New Testament message (see 1 John 1.1; Acts 10.39).

In our sermons, the hearers should be reflected and should be heard to speak for themselves. They may well be better at Christian reflecting than the professional preachers are. The liberation theologians of Latin America asserted, 'We are writing about the dreams of the people, and it is from their wisdom that we get our theology.' So we meet people where they are and echo their questions – even if we have no answers. We can do this only if we spend time understanding their society, values and personal situations. This is called 'auditing', or 'networking', and there are techniques for doing this systematically (see Bowen, 1996:172, 199–203).

A Dramatic Event

When John Wesley preached, often to big crowds in the open air, he was conscious of playing his part in a drama which was being directed by God for a particular purpose (see p. 6). Wesley could not know what that purpose was. He was like a spectator, who would eventually discover what God was doing in this drama. God often blesses people through bad sermons more than through good ones (see p. 32). This comes as a surprise to those who are just beginning their public ministry, but they soon learn that God fulfils his purposes through their words in ways which they had never planned. In any case, the key to communication is not words, but love.

This is why Karl Barth did not like to apply his message specifically to the lives of his hearers. He liked to leave them with the message of the word of God because, he said, 'only the Holy Spirit knows how it is to be worked out in the lives of his people, and that is his work, not mine.' However, it is wise normally to make suggestions throughout the sermon of ways in which the message might work out in people's lives, but to remember that we have only a very partial understanding of the purposes of God and the situation of the people. We must leave it to them to discover through reflection and prayer what the message means for them, and pray that God will lead them to greater wisdom and obedience than we can show them. Bishop Festo Kivengere often took part in evangelistic missions with colleagues who wanted to issue an appeal for people to 'come forward' or to register their response in a visible way. But he had reservations about this: 'better they go home and reflect, then they will respond as God wants, not as I want' (Coomes, 1990:255).

Wesley and Barth wanted their hearers to pay more attention to the message than to the preacher. However, the sermon is you because, however much you want to hide behind Christ and his word, 'It is the man to whom one is listening, not the words he is saying', according to Cardinal Basil Hume. When God gave Ezekiel the scroll, the prophet had to eat it himself before he could declare it to others. Taking God's message into the world is the human counterpart of God's action in the incarnation. When God became human, he sat where his hearers sat, especially in the stories he told, about farming, trading and looking for lost things. Jesus did this not only to affirm but also to challenge and change the assumptions his hearers had never questioned. 'Things don't have to be like this', he told them.

Anyone who translates a message from one language into another becomes involved in the learning process. The same is true of preachers, who first receive the text themselves and then make it 'incarnate'. This means they 'translate' it into the context of the hearers. Preachers become learners, as they enter the world of the hearers. In the words of Augustine,

> When people are affected by us as we speak and we by them as they learn, we dwell in one another and thus both they, as it were, speak in us what they hear, while we, after a fashion, learn in them what we teach. (Walker, 2002:228; see also Sanneh, 1989:179)

In sermons, preacher and people share together their experience of God's work in Christ and in them.

The disabled student mentioned on p. 10 has recently been ordained a pastor. It is not easy for people to understand what he is saying when he preaches. They have to concentrate. But doing this brings them unexpected blessing. Those who work hard at listening get more out of it, and especially when they are listening to someone who has experienced more suffering than any of them. He might have good reason to be angry with God about his disability, but God has given him the gifts of faith and patience, and he inspires others to trust the Lord.

Special Note B
A GUIDE FOR ASSESSMENT

To Church, and there being a lazy preacher, I slept out the sermon.

Samuel Pepys

The best way to develop the skills of preaching is to evaluate your sermon face to face with friends who want to support you. It is not easy to do this, because preachers always feel vulnerable, sensitive and fearful of criticism after preaching. But any assessment needs to take place either immediately after preaching or by tape-recording your sermon and listening to it later. Here are three models for assessment:

1 *By you, after listening to your sermon on tape*

(a) What was the aim, and was it clear throughout?
(b) Do you notice any mannerisms, repetitions or peculiarities in voice or style?
(c) Did the opening remarks capture and hold the attention?
(d) Did the sermon
   (i) expound scripture; and
   (ii) relate to people's lives?
(e) How effective were the illustrations, examples, word-pictures, stories, etc.?
(f) Did the ending effectively drive home the point of the message?
(g) How well integrated was the sermon with the worship in the service?
(h) How did the sermon affect your own life and thought?

Or you could ask yourself:

(a) Did the spoken word (the sermon) uplift the living word (Christ), expound the written word (the Scriptures) and find support in the symbolic word (the congregation)?
(b) Did your words speak to their minds, hearts and wills, as Paul described in Romans 6.17? Did it make them:
   (i) think and learn?
   (ii) feel moved?
   (iii) want to take action?

2 *By you, with a friendly guide or supervisor*

The above questions can be the headings for the discussion you have with your friend. Your friend should raise further matters, such as:

(a) Describe in detail how you prepared this sermon – e.g. why, where, when, how long?
(b) What reading did you do as part of your preparation?
(c) What experiences, observations or reflections on life contributed to your preparation?

The friendliest and wisest critic a preacher ever has is likely to be their wife or husband. A bishop was one day told by his wife, 'You spoiled that message because you were shouting too much.'

3 *By the congregation, with you*

This should not be regarded as an assessment. It is instead an opportunity for the congregation to reflect on the message, and share the ways in which it spoke to them. Often the reaction of an ordinary congregation is more valuable than an evaluation by an expert.

(a) What was the main point, and was it clear throughout?
(b) Could you hear the preacher clearly?
(c) Was the preacher's delivery varied and interesting, so as to hold your attention?
(d) Did you learn anything new? Did any part strike you as specially true or relevant?
(e) Were there any parts of it which you found hard to follow?
(f) Did you have any questions about the sermon, or things you disagreed with?
(g) Were you led into and out of the text and returned to your own situation?
(h) Was the sermon too short – or too long?
(i) What illustrations, or visual aids, did you find particularly helpful?
(j) What are you taking away with you as a result of hearing this sermon?

The last question is the most important. One preacher had four people keep 'sermon diaries' of their reflections, which gave him feedback from the pews, because the important thing is not what the preacher says, but what the people hear. The hearers are always right, for the sermon ends with them, not with the speaker. 'Yes, but what did it *do*?' we should finally ask – and perhaps only God will ever fully know the answer to that question. One person will want to learn more and join a Bible study group or read a book. Another will realize the need to apologize to a friend, and even make restitution. Another will feel called to help those in need.

Above everything else, a sermon should be simple and clear. The gospel has power *because* it is simple. Richard Baxter wrote that the work of pastors was most often spoiled by the sin of pride:

Pride chooses our company, decides what clothes we shall wear, and even what books we study and what degrees we take. It chooses the subjects of our sermons and the language we use. God tells us to be serious and simple, so as to carry conviction and change people's lives; but pride persuades us to paint the window so as to dim the light; to be clever rather than clear. Pride goes with us into the pulpit and tells us to amuse and entertain in order to receive people's praise for our learning or our eloquence. Then when we go home, pride is still with us, making us worry whether people liked our preaching instead of asking God to use his word to change people's lives. Even worse, pride makes us envy our colleagues when they are praised more than us – we prefer people to criticize them so that we appear in a better light. (1950:95, adapted)

Study Suggestions

1 Look again at the definitions of preaching (pp. 37, 41–2). Of all the expressions used, which best describe preaching, in your opinion? Finally, write your own definition.

2 'The one-person sermon to a silent congregation should be a thing of the past.' What is your opinion of the arguments supporting this idea on p. 38?

3 What 'authority' does the Christian preacher have, and where does it come from?

4 In what ways, if any, should preachers try to 'entertain' people?

5 What experience do you have of:

(a) 'hot' and
(b) 'cool' communication?

Which is more appropriate:

(a) for you personally?
(b) for the culture in which you live?

6 In what ways was Paul's style of speaking and writing affected by the nature of the people he was addressing? See Acts 17.16–31; Colossians 2.6–23; Romans 3.1–9; 6.1–4.

7 What prevents people from reacting to or asking questions of the preacher?

8 What experience have you had of congregations having a major effect on sermons?

9 Why might suffering make people lose faith in God? How can preachers help such people?

10 Ask yourself the questions in Special Note B, section 1, about any sermon which has held your attention recently.

11 Next time you preach, gather together some of the congregation, and ask them some of the questions in section 3 on p. 49. But don't argue with them, just listen! Which of their comments surprised you? What did you learn? If possible, get a friend to help you evaluate their comments.

12 What were the aims of Puritan preachers? What good advice do you find in the quotations from the Puritan Richard Baxter on pp. 24 and 50?

4

INDIRECT PREACHING

'But why do you hate stories so much?' Haroun blurted, feeling stunned. 'Stories are fun . . .'

'The world, however, is not for Fun,' Khattam-Shud replied. 'The world is for controlling.'

'Which world?' Haroun made himself ask.

'Your world, my world, all worlds,' came the reply. 'They are all there to be Ruled. And inside every single story, inside every Stream in the Ocean, there lies a world, a story-world, that I cannot Rule at all. And that is the reason why.'

Salman Rushdie, *Haroun and the Sea of Stories*, 1990

'The Bible is a pictorial book', wrote the late Bishop Festo Kivengere. He is said to have preached 'like a child throwing paints with his fingers all at once onto a canvas in great excitement'. Like him, preachers should use all the different images, pictorial language and illustrations available to them. Many of these are found in the Bible text itself, and many of them lie within our own history and culture. Preaching in the Bible includes fables, histories, legends, debates (dialogues), interviews, poetry, dramas, visual aids, sacraments, allegories, congregational responses. Our preaching should also be like this. If it is, it will not only instruct but also 'delight and convince' the hearers, as St Augustine said it should. This chapter contains some examples of these 'indirect' forms of preaching.

Stories

All cultures have stories which are handed down from generation to generation. Many of them are told not because they are literally true, but because they contain truth in the form of a story. Jesus' parables were like this, and so are many African fables, which are often about animals who meet and talk with one another and with human beings. They all teach valuable lessons about how people should live their lives. See Special Note C.

An African traditional story tells of a poor man who travelled with a prince and a rich merchant to a far country in the hope of marrying a king's daughter. On their journey, they met first a crocodile, then some birds, then an ant and finally a fly, all of whom asked for help in different ways. The two rich men angrily refused, but the poor man gave them what they needed until he had nothing left and had to become the slave of his companions. When they got to the king's palace, they were each given hard tasks to earn the right to marry the princess. The prince and the merchant failed, but the poor man was helped in turn by those he had helped on the road and miraculously won the lady's hand in marriage (see Muhando, 1962:65).

The New Testament also has a story about foreigners travelling a long way to see a king. They brought gifts and established a relationship with the newborn King, whereas the rich king who was fellow-countryman with the baby King hated him and tried to kill him. This story was probably told by Matthew because it was for him a picture of his own Church fellowship, which consisted of many poor Jews and non-Jews (Gentiles). They had accepted Jesus as Messiah and met regularly to worship him, whereas many of the Jewish religious leaders had rejected him completely.

The morals of these two simple stories are different from one another, but each has its own message for us, which preachers can use effectively. Whether the event actually happened does not matter so much as the truth which each story enshrines. A story-teller is like an artist who paints the Last Supper to communicate with his particular audience who may be medieval European or Palestinian, Indian or African. He paints Jesus and the Twelve not as they really were, but as today's audience would see them (see p. 63). Over half the Bible is story, and the Gospels consist mostly of dialogue and stories. No doubt the authors realized that their readers were most likely to understand and respond if they told them the stories of what Jesus did and said.

The black culture of America developed the tradition of skilfully turning Bible stories into forms which were specifically suitable for their own oppressed people:

> Young folks, old folks, everybody come
> To the darkies' Sunday school and make yourself at home.
> Bring your sticks of chewing gum and sit upon the floor,
> And hear some Bible stories that you've never heard before.

They used visual language to enable their hearers to imagine the freedom and deliverance which God can bring to an enslaved people. These stories told by black preachers did not teach the people *what* to think by explaining doctrine – they showed them *how* to think. 'Black preachers penetrate into the subconscious of their hearers more successfully than white because they are more concerned with art than argument. They express themselves in terms of stories' (Mitchell, 1977:32). They are aware of the effect they are having and they respond to the congregation's response.

When telling a story, focus on the characters, describe the place and the time, show what movements are taking place, use direct speech to show what the characters are feeling, make the most of moments of suspense and of surprise. Try not to explain the moral at the end. A story is like a poem or painting – it should speak for itself, leaving listeners to think and work it out. But you may want to indicate parallels with our situation today. If so, interweave them into the story, saying, 'It's just like . . .', or even 'It's not like . . .' So the pattern of story-telling is story-reflection-story-reflection, etc.

Imagination

We find the writers of the Bible sometimes letting their imagination loose on a text. See how the writer of Hebrews 5.1–10 lets his imagination play with Psalm 110 and Genesis 14.18–20. Jesus' imagination created characters such as the rich man and Lazarus. In his story of the Good Samaritan, we 'see' in our imagination the wine, the oil, the inn, the donkey, the two coins. In the same way Muslims in the Sufi tradition have often told imaginative stories, like the following from the Sufi Attar of Nishapur in the twelfth century: 'Some Israelites reviled Jesus one day, but He answered by saying prayers for them. "You prayed for them," said a bystander. "Weren't you angry?" Jesus replied, "I could spend only what I had in my purse"' (Wijngaards, 1978:169).

A preacher could reflect in imagination on Jesus' words in John 6.12: 'Gather the fragments left over, so that nothing may be lost', and preach a sermon on them which showed that God wants nothing he has created to be wasted – not even the person who feels ugly, poor, stupid, useless and sinful. All such people may feel they have nothing to offer Jesus except their failures – but he wants to use such people in the world to serve him.

Legends

Some stories are legends which tribes and clans treasure as their own heritage. These are always very powerful means of communication, and can often be linked up with the myths or stories we find in the Bible. On Easter Day 1939, in KwaZulu, South Africa, in the town cemetery, the Revd Michael Mzobe preached on the Valley of Dry

Bones (Ezekiel 37). Standing among the graves, this is what he said (Sundkler, 1960:283f.):

> In the beginning God created everything – even man in his own image. But Adam fell and death and disaster came into the world. After his death he was given an honoured place in Paradise, sitting all by himself on a balcony. From his balcony he followed the history of humankind. He saw his own son murder his brother, and there on the balcony he had to cry out in sorrow and shame, 'Ah! my guilt, my great guilt!' And then the Flood came, but people went about in their sin and forgetfulness of their God. They were overtaken by the flood waters and were all caught up in terror – and Adam, in Paradise, overcome by sorrow had to cry, 'My guilt, my great guilt!' [All the dramatic events of Bible history passed in review for his Zulu hearers . . .] Generation after generation was born on earth, only to sin and die – for the sake of Adam's sin. You Zulus, consider that heavy weight of sorrow on the heart of our Great Ancestor Adam; all that suffering all for his sin's sake!
>
> But Zulus, men and women, consider that incredible joy which filled Adam's heart on the first Easter morning as the Hero of Heaven came in through the Gate of Heaven, with His crown of thorns, now a brilliant crown of victory, walking straight up to the Throne of the Almighty. There He gave his report that from this day Satan and sin and death had been overcome. For now He, the Second Adam, had won the victory.
>
> And the first Adam had peace.

There are many parallels between the stories in the Hebrew Bible and African myths going back to the dawn of time. Mzobe brought these two worlds together in a way which riveted the attention of his Zulu hearers, not least because the place was the cemetery where the ancestors lay, and the time was Easter Day. Mzobe regarded Christ as 'Adam's Resurrector' – a concept worthy of one of the great patristic theologians, but especially relevant for Zulus because it also begins to face the question which the missionaries usually avoided, 'What about our ancestors – what is their fate? Did Christ redeem them?' Preachers cannot afford to avoid questions which the people are asking.

Sometimes the local culture has a word which gives a clear picture of what the Bible is saying. For example, all young Masai men belong to the sacred brotherhood of their age group – i.e. all those who are circumcised within a seven-year period – and are given a name never to be repeated. This is called the *orporor*, and the Masai chose this as their translation of the word 'Church', 'but', they said, 'this Orporor is not just for 7 years nor just for Masai men but for all people from the beginning to the end of time. It will be the first Universal Brotherhood' (Donovan, 1978:93). It consists of people and could never be thought of as a building!

Dialogue

This is a very common mode of encounter in the Bible. Jesus constantly challenged his hearers with questions which drew them into dialogue with him. This is the way the prophets felt that God spoke to them (Isaiah 1.18; Ezekiel 2.1), and the way they spoke to their hearers (Jeremiah 37.17ff.; Malachi 3.8–13). One of the biggest faults in much modern preaching is that it is a monologue. It is, however, possible to conduct dialogue on various levels. If members of the congregation are known to be expert in a certain field, then the preacher will be wise to give them an opportunity to speak more authoritatively about that subject than the preacher can, by giving them advance warning of questions he will put to them. Or two conflicting viewpoints can be set up in the form of a dialogue. Some texts lend themselves to this kind of treatment. One example is the contrasting viewpoints of the 'weak' and the 'strong' brother in Romans 14, which is not easy to explain in words but could be turned into a dialogue or a drama, which is easy to grasp. Or the preacher can give the congregation real involvement in the sermon by asking them to think and to respond before he draws out the teaching of the texts. Here is one simple example.

The parish Church of St Martha the Housewife is situated in one of the poorest districts of the city of Nottingham. Often you will not find anyone in church who has a regular job. The vicar, John Harding, used to include the congregation actively in his preaching. Here is an extract from one of his sermons. He wrote the days of the week on a flip chart and then wrote on the chart the way the people responded about each day:

Vicar: Joan, which day do you like best?

Joan: Saturday . . . Sunday.

Vicar: You like the Sunday. Grace, which day do you like best?

Grace: Tuesday.

Vicar: Tuesday! Why Tuesday?

Grace: It's pension day.

Vicar: Pension day! I like Tuesday, too, because it's my day off – but I like Sunday too, you know. Good. In the reading that we had, Mary of Magdala came to the tomb on which day?

Many: Sunday.

Vicar: . . . came on the Sunday, but for the Jewish people, their festival day wasn't a Sunday at all. What was it?

Many: Saturday.

Vicar: Saturday. And so the Jewish Monday morning would have been which day?

Many: Sunday.

Vicar: Sunday. We like the holy days and the special days but the Mondays dip right down. And what God did was take the despised Monday morning, if you can think of Sunday being a Monday morning for the Jewish people, and he made it so holy and special. Well, he will do that for everything you find so difficult to come to terms with . . .

John Harding used to say he was never quite sure where the sermon would take him because he did not know how people would respond. This makes for a special Sunday experience. The sermon can even get slightly out of control as a result of disagreement or unpredictable answers, but it is actually a sign of growth and strength when we can disagree together within the community. We are, after all, a priesthood of *all* believers.

In England, it is the congregations in the inner-city, poorer districts who are most responsive to this type of sermon. Affluent people, with professional jobs, are often embarrassed to speak out and prefer to be 'well-behaved' in church. They are often less responsive than their fellow-believers who are poorer or more troubled by the problems of life.

Some of the earliest preaching in Africa took the form of dialogue. A Yoruba catechist, W. S. Allen in Ibadan, found that he was constantly reacting to parables or stories told by the people, most of them not yet Christians. In 1873 an old man asked if he could respond to the sermon and told of a man with three sons, named Poison, Fire and Covetousness. They were arguing among themselves about who was greatest. Poison claimed he had most power, but his father said, 'No, there is always an antidote to you.' Fire then made a similar claim, but again the father said, 'No, a quantity of water will defeat you.' But when Covetousness spoke, his father replied, 'Yes, you live deep within people, and nothing can defeat you.' In the same region in 1860, Joseph Smith talked to the people in their own way and found that often they gave him a text from which to preach and 'having produced the text, will the more willingly listen' (Peel, 2000:161). To preach like this is both to take risks and to rely on the Holy Spirit rather than our own preparation – but dialogue has a special sort of life which is often absent from carefully prepared texts. It may not be so effective as a medium of teaching.

Interview

In many parts of the world today, the 'chat show' captures large audiences on TV. People love to 'listen in' to the stories of other people's lives. Many of the ancient fables, told round the campfire at night, were just as popular in earlier days. This is a medium of communication which is especially suitable for use in church services. It can be a little like an extended dialogue. Interviews fall into a number of different categories:

1 As mentioned above, it is a good way of making use of the expertise of members of the congregation. They may not feel equipped to preach like the pastor, but they could sit at the front and answer questions about matters of which they have specialist knowledge. Interviewing such a person calls for special skills also. The interviewer must be totally absorbed not in the audience but in the person being interviewed, for it is that person's wisdom and experience which people want to hear – not the interviewer's. But the interviewer needs also to be aware of the audience, to ask the sort of questions they would wish to put to the interviewee if they were doing the asking. A private – often intimate – conversation is taking place; and the congregation is eavesdropping.

2 Perhaps the person being interviewed has no specialist knowledge, but just has a story to tell. Perhaps she is a new member of the congregation who has just come to live in town – this is a good way of briefly introducing her. Perhaps she is a missionary – nurse, teacher, carer – who has been serving God in another country or culture, and comes to report back to the congregation. If she feels unable to preach, her message can be communicated just as well, perhaps better, by means of an interview. Or maybe a member of the congregation has a testimony to give about the way God has met with him, answered prayer, or changed his life in some way (see p. 46). We should not keep these experiences to ourselves: 'Let the redeemed of the LORD say so, those he redeemed from trouble' (Psalm 107.2).

3 Sometimes Christian people feel that God is leading them to speak a word of prophecy. This can be called 'a word of wisdom'. It takes the form of a conviction that we need to take action to correct something that is wrong. A sister in an Indian Christian school pointed out that teachers were showing favouritism to the children from rich families – they got better marks, less punishment, more privileges and more promotion than poor children. Quoting Luke 14.13, she said it should be the poor and backward who are given any special favours. Pastors should be ready to include within their sermons contributions such as this from lay people. If a word of prophecy like this is to be allowed, we should be sure that it has the following four features:
    (a) a Christian value which is in danger of being lost;
    (b) relevance to a specific situation;

(c) the judgement of God;
(d) support from the Bible.

Drama

There are very many types of drama, and many drama resource-books have been published or are available on the Web. The type most commonly seen in all parts of the Church is the nativity play. It is often done by children in school or Sunday school at Christmas, but it is based on the mystery plays of the Middle Ages, which have been part of the Church's teaching and evangelistic ministry for many generations. Not only the story of Christmas, but many other Bible stories can come to life if they are read dramatically, with or without actions. Preachers can use *The Dramatic Bible* or, much better, themselves turn the reading into a dramatic form.

The events following the resurrection have been put into a dramatic form by Stuart Jackman in his book *The Davidson Affair* (1966). He imagines that the Imperial Television Corporation in Rome has heard rumours of 'More Trouble in the Middle East' and has decided to send its special correspondent to cover the story. The correspondent interviews the characters who have seen (or have not seen) something – Pontius Pilate, the Revd Jacob Nicodemus, Zacchaeus, the Magdala, Thomas Didymus, Mr Cleopas, Lord Caiaphas, etc. The ancient story is translated into modern idiom, which helps people to look at it through fresh eyes. Any part of it could be dramatically presented in church at Easter. In the same way an ancient Chinese writer, Ssu-ma Ch'ien (145–85 BC), brought history to life by recording it in the form of character-sketches of maligned statesmen, rash generals and assassins (Wijngaards, 1978:119). The Bible is full of characters (e.g. Gideon, Barnabas) ready to be brought to life.

Drama can be combined with stories. Adults and children can play parts in the telling of the story. They can speak the words of the characters, or they can mime the actions without saying anything, while the narrator tells the story.

Ignatius of Loyola, in his *Spiritual Exercises*, encouraged his followers, when reading Bible stories, to imagine themselves as one or other of the characters in those stories (see Nouwen, 1994:5). We can use this technique in our preaching, by allowing a few minutes of silence and inviting our hearers to imagine how they would feel if they were one of the characters involved in the story. They can then share out loud how they feel, or how they would respond in that situation. In this way, they become part of the sermon and discover how the Bible speaks to them directly.

Everyday life can be presented in dramatic forms. This can be done by a prepared script, as is usually the case in the Western world, but many people in India and Africa are specially gifted at doing this without any prepared script. The preacher can outline a real-life situation, and then the actors will create an imaginary scene, making up the words as they go along. The message of God in the situation can be either included in the drama or left to the preacher to explain at the end.

One other art form which must be included under the category of drama is dance. This skill is well developed in almost every culture of the world. Energetic and acrobatic dance with music is used for evangelism in many parts of Africa. Quieter forms have been developed in Asia and in the Western world. The movement and music conveys to the spectators the same meanings which are contained in the words of Scripture.

Poetry

Preachers do not always recognize poetry when it is in front of them; they certainly find it difficult to use it in communicating with their congregations. But the Bible is full of poetry. This is mentioned several times in this Guide, but it is worth saying a little about poetry at this point. Poetry takes many different forms in different cultures, and believers have always been prepared to put Christian content into secular, non-Christian art-forms which they have encountered. Exodus 15 and Psalm 29 probably took over forms of poetry which the Israelites encountered in the land. Jesus' parables are full of poetic passages, which have been expertly analysed by Kenneth Bailey (1983).

Proverbs, usually in poetic or rhythmic forms, are central to the thought of many societies. When used in sermons, they create vivid pictures in people's minds and relate to the world in which they live. All cultures related to the Semitic tradition – such as Hebrew, Arabic, Swahili – have a rich storehouse of proverbs. The Revd W. Salter Price urged all his readers who wished to become effective preachers to the people of East Africa to

> diligently study this collection of proverbs; make a selection of the most telling; get at their real gist; and then store them in your memory, for use as occasion may serve. 'Because the preacher was wise, he gave good heed, and sought out, and set in order, many proverbs.' (Taylor, 1891:vii)

See also Mark 4.25 and 1 John 5.1, both of which might well have been popular sayings on the street.

Music

Ever since the Psalms, music has been a divinely sanctioned means of helping God's people to grow spiritually. The antiphonal (alternately by two groups) form used then is also used within many African traditions. Such traditions as these need to be reflected in our worship today, as they have been in the liturgy of the Anglican Church in Kenya. The preacher can use these forms. Just as Charles Wesley 'baptized' secular tunes for use in his great hymns, so the black slaves of the new world baptized into Christian worship the forms of song which they had brought from their African homelands, and they gained world renown as 'Negro spirituals'. Martin Luther King Jr, leader of the Civil Rights Movement in the USA, wrote, 'The freedom songs are playing a strong and vital role in our struggle. They give the people new courage and a sense of unity.' John Newton, rector, and William Cowper, poet, worked together to entice the parishioners of the English village of Olney to attend the prayer meeting by promising them 'a brand new song' every week. Among these were 'Amazing grace' and 'How sweet the name of Jesus sounds', still favourite hymns today.

Roberta King (2004:293–300) has described how a large group of Senufo Christians from different clans in the Cote d'Ivoire gathered for a workshop to compose new songs for the church. 'We are here,' they said, 'to learn how to sing in the language of our ethnic group . . . we know we have great richness there.' Their aim was to set the story of Abraham to song. They finished up with 47 new songs. Here is a part of one of them, from the Nyarafolo clan:

And Abraham took his son and went to the mountain!
He took Isaac and went to the mountain!
A new thing is here! Listen, peoples! Listen Nyarafolos!
  Abraham, listen you all . . .
  Abraham, God talked with him!
  And God said,
    'Take the covenant child, the one I gave you
    Take that child, the covenant one.
    And give him to me.
    Take him to the mountain!'

The ideas expressed here are contrary to traditional Senufo religion. For example, the Senufo think God is distant and unapproachable and does not talk with human beings, and that blessings come to them by following their parents' custom of worshipping the spirits. They are unlikely to change their views by being taught new theological ideas in abstract language. But the process of composing and singing songs about Abraham to local Senufo music will help them to receive, as a group, the covenant promises of the God of Abraham, in a way that makes sense in their culture. They will be able to see for themselves what God is really like.

Visual Aids

The English art critic, John Ruskin, wrote:

> Great nations write their autobiographies in three manuscripts, the book of their deeds, the book of their words and the book of their art. Not one of these books can be understood unless we read the two others, but of the three the only trustworthy one is the last. (Clark 1969:1)

By 'art' he meant drawings, paintings, sculpture, architecture, i.e. conveying ideas and culture by means of visual images, as all human beings have done from the very earliest times. All sorts of art can be used in preaching, but here are some particular examples.

1 *Posters*

Posters have been used in many parts of the world to draw people's attention to a new message. The first Burmese Christian minister ever to be commissioned was Maung Ing, who went off alone down the coast at Tavoy in 1837. He laboriously painted Christian banners which he displayed on the front of his house to attract passers-by, and so became one of the pioneers of poster evangelism (Maung Shwe Wa, 1963:58). An even simpler form was developed by James Read in Yorubaland in 1877. It was called *The Wordless Book*. It had four double pages coloured black, red, white and gold. These 'happened' to fit in with Yoruba symbolism of black for what is negative, red for danger or mediation and white for positive spirituality. The people readily saw it as illustrating sin, redemption, sanctification and glory, and they responded in large numbers. One man said, 'Now, the truth has come!' (Peel, 2000:168f.).

Today the use of posters has been developed in Latin America, especially by Paulo Freire of Brazil (Freire, 1972:77–93; Berryman, 1987:35f.). They are used especially for communicating with illiterate people, but are equally useful for the educated. The aim is to raise people's consciousness by using images which highlight real issues they face day by day. A poster may show people building a house or harvesting a crop. The leader simply asks, 'What do we see here?' and the discussion gets progressively livelier – but led by the people themselves. They 'decode' the picture, identify their problems and generate solutions. It can be done with pictures of Bible scenes (e.g.

Rembrandt's *The Return of the Prodigal Son*, 'decoded' by Henri Nouwen in his book of that name), or of church situations, imaginatively developed by Roman Catholics at the Lumko Institute in Johannesburg. This gives people a leadership role in ministry, rather like 'Dialogue' (p. 56 above), with the result that they own it for themselves, even though preachers may need to say clearly what the people have said. China's Mao Zedong said, 'We must teach the masses clearly what we have received from them confusedly.'

The National Gallery in London presented an exhibition of paintings to mark the millennium year of 2000. The director, Neil MacGregor, called it 'Seeing Salvation' and compiled a book about it called *The Image of Christ*. Huge crowds went to 'see' the same gospel which they hear in church, but presented in new and creative ways through inscriptions, paintings and sculpture from the fourth century to the present time. It proved to be a powerful method of evangelization. In the same way, the ancient Eastern churches used icons to convey a message which illiterate people could easily understand. For example, in the Armenian Church a set of icons painted in 989 AD shows the wise men of Matthew 2 dressed in trousers, jacket, coat, pearls and fluttering ribbons. This identifies them with the Zoroastrian priests of that time, so that 'the priests of the old religion might be shown acknowledging a higher priesthood by worshipping the Christ Child' (Haleblian, 2004:322).

2 *Symbolic action*

The Bible is full of actions which not only dramatize a message, but also seem to impart power to it. The most important of these are the sacraments (p. 67), but the prophets also regarded actions as having even more power than words to reveal God's message. The images belong to ordinary, daily life, like an almond branch and a cooking pot (Jeremiah 1), but speak in new ways of spiritual values. See Jeremiah 13 and 19 and Hosea 1 and 3, which seem to have made specially challenging demands on the prophets themselves.

Symbolic actions, in the form of 'signs and wonders', were an essential part of the ministry of Jesus. One-fifth of the stories in Luke's Gospel tell us of the miracles he did, especially miracles of healing. These were signs showing who he was and authenticating his preaching. This ministry continued in the early Church and continues today in Pentecostal and charismatic churches. They help the Church in its evangelism because people see the results of faith before they can fully understand it. This has been called 'power evangelism', and many books have been written about this form of ministry – some supporting it and some criticizing it. See, for example, Bowen, 1996:160–8.

Preachers today can generate interest, and probably response, by using symbolic actions at certain points. Here are some examples:

(a) *The Holy Spirit* is both a gift given *to* people and also a gift which flows *out of* them, as in John 7.38 (the Jews' water-festival, see commentaries). The preacher takes a glass and a jug. For the glass to be of any use, it must be filled with water. That is as it should be, nice and comfortable. But the preacher, like God, does not stop; he continues pouring until it overflows out of the glass onto the floor. That's what the Spirit is supposed to be like in our lives – the water does indeed come from the glass (us) but originates from the jug (God); it can't overflow to others until it has first filled us; and it makes an awful mess on the floor – the Holy Spirit causes uncomfortable disturbances around us.

(b) *Faith*: Often we wonder if our faith is strong enough. But the direction of our faith is more important than its strength. If we rely on Christ, the strength is his, not ours. This can be symbolized by two chairs. Both look similar, but one is broken and will collapse if anyone sits on it. The preacher can invite two young people to come and sit on the chairs. When one of them falls, the preacher criticizes him for the weakness of his faith. But actually it will be obvious to everyone that it was the chair which was at fault, not the youngster – and the point has been made.

3 *Overhead projector and PowerPoint*

OHPs and PowerPoint are sometimes used in churches instead of hymn books, but can also be of use to the preacher and can clarify the points of a sermon. They should be used to present symbols and diagrams – and should probably not be used every Sunday. It should also be remembered that the primary aim of sermons is not to teach but to inspire and move to action – though teaching is often an important step in that process.

Words should be used sparingly on OHPs and PowerPoint, as on posters. The value of visuals is that they enable people to *see* with their eyes the same message they are *hearing* with their ears. Many people are more receptive to images than to words. If words are used, they should be few, e.g. headings of main points as in a lecture, and they should be combined with the image or the diagram.

4 *Features of local interest*

Many of these are ready to hand. It may be nothing more elaborate than a tree or stream which has a story or tradition attached to it. It may be an eclipse of the moon or the sun. Some features are especially to be found in cities and in city churches. These are often memorials which remind us of a person or an event. If the story of the person or event is told well, then the message will renew itself in people's minds whenever they see the memorial – which many of them may do every Sunday. Here are some such examples:

Outside All Saints Cathedral, Nairobi, is a small bridge which everyone has to cross to enter the cathedral. On it is a small memorial to Captain Ryall, who was killed by a man-eating lion in 1899. He was helping to build the Uganda Railway from the coast to the Great Lakes, and was lying in wait to shoot the lion, which had already killed many of the workers. He bravely gave his life so that others might be able to travel in safety and comfort into the heart of Africa. There is an obvious parallel between his self-sacrifice and the offering of Jesus on the cross so that we might be able to pass safely through this world to our heavenly destination. But the cathedral congregation who heard that story would now remember not only Captain Ryall but also the sacrificial love of Jesus every time they crossed the bridge.

Visitors to the Cathedral Church of the Redemption, New Delhi, can see a stained-glass window with three panels. The bottom panel is a picture of chaos and disorder in the form of a whirlpool which sucks you down. But the cross of St Thomas in the centre panel shines down on the disorder, offering you the hope of being lifted up by the redeeming power of Christ to the top panel. There, colour and orderliness show love and purpose leading to the gold of glory and the white of peace. This is available for all, for the cross radiates outward to embrace every part of the created order in God's love. This window could provide the theme of one or many sermons.

Many of the ancient cathedrals of Europe have stories in stone, or in glass, especially useful in an age when few people could read. Even today the preacher in Norwich Cathedral has only to look upwards to see the whole story of salvation carved in hundreds of colourful stone bosses on the ceiling, from the creation in Genesis 1 to the Day of Pentecost and the Day of Judgment. It's a ready-made visual aid, adapted to almost any sermon you could preach!

5   *Use of films*

Films are one of the most popular forms of entertainment throughout the world. Some of these are feature films shown in cinemas; some are videos made for TV; some are soap operas telling stories about ordinary people, like *Neighbours* in Australia or *EastEnders* in the UK. Quite a lot of these films reflect the issues which people are facing in their lives – just the sort of situations, in fact, which Jesus addressed in his ministry in the Gospels. Preachers would do well to follow his example by linking their sermons to the themes of these films. There are different ways of doing this.

The Church of St Gabriel's, Liverpool, has developed this kind of ministry. There is no cinema in the poor district of St Gabriel's, but once a month a film, suitable for families and often chosen by them, is shown in church. A family pays £1 admission fee. The vicar, Malcolm Rogers, says that in this way the church is subsidizing entertainment for people who have not got much money. The following Sunday the vicar preaches on the film. Films which have been shown recently include *Finding Nemo*, *Harry Potter* films, and *The Grinch that Stole Christmas*. These are all secular films suitable for children and adults in the UK. They may not communicate so well in some other cultures. Churches which do not have the facilities of St Gabriel's could ask members of the congregations either to pass round videos of old films or to watch one or two episodes of a soap opera on TV the week before the service.

The film *Finding Nemo* is all about a young fish who became impatient with home life, got into bad company and eventually swam away from home. His father went desperately looking for him. The film shows the adventures of the naughty fish and also of his loving father. It is like a fishy parallel to the parable of the Prodigal Son. A sermon could begin by asking people what they remember from the film, and then picking up some of these responses and reflecting on them. Have any of us ever made any journeys away from God? What might stop Nemo from thinking he could ever go back home? Pieces of paper may then be handed out to the congregation, on which they may write down anything that they have felt which stops them from enjoying God's love in his family – maybe divorce, unkindnesses, crime, sins. In St Gabriel's, they fold the paper tightly and throw it on the ground in the centre aisle of the church. They leave it there, and later in the service they all stand up and go to the back of the church, walking over the bits of paper, and leaving them behind. They return to their places by going back down the side aisles. The vicar picks up all the papers and burns them outside the church.

The sermon is not given all at once, but in short sound bites, interspersed with suitable songs, readings, prayers and contributions from the congregation. Young children are given paper drawings on the theme to colour in. Life is a struggle for many of these poor people. It is not easy for them to listen to a long sermon but, just as they read tabloid newspapers, they can easily manage a sermon built on visual material and broken up into short sound bites. This form of preaching is so popular in the parish that they have been inviting their friends to come along. Going to church is not only their duty; it is also fun.

Preachers, of course, cannot know what responses they will get from the congregation. They must respond to whatever people might say, and be ready to use several different approaches to the film or to the Bible story. Sometimes an evangelistic theme will emerge – or one relating to ethical behaviour, spiritual growth or doctrine. Whatever it may be, the ministry will not be the preacher's alone; it will be shared with the people. But they will be helped to make links between the issues of daily life and the biblical text – because preachers must not lose sight of the aim, which is that God shall speak his word to people as they are today.

There is a different kind of film which aims to be directly informative, moving and evangelistic. The well-known *Jesus* film, which has been shown all over the world and dubbed into hundreds of different languages, is the clearest example. The Hollywood film by Mel Gibson, *The Passion of the Christ* (2004) is also being used as a means of evangelism.

6 *Using newscasts*

The same principle can be applied to newscasts in societies where most people have access to TV. If something of local interest has been watched by large numbers of people, then it can be used as the basis of the sermon. In certain dramatic cases, it may be *essential* to refer to that event in the sermon, as when Princess Diana was killed or when the *Herald of Free Enterprise* sank, both of which happened on a Saturday evening (see pp. 5, 9). A less dramatic event was featured on South African TV when President Nelson Mandela left the country on an official visit with his vice-president, and handed over executive authority to Chief Mangosuthu Buthelezi. This was significant because Buthelezi had often given Mandela a lot of trouble by opposing him in Parliament. Buthelezi responded by thanking Mandela effusively for showing such confidence in him, in spite of his past troublesomeness. This could be made into a vivid picture of how God entrusts to us the task of representing him and ministering for him, in spite of the many times we have failed him in the past.

The Sacraments

Baptism and the Eucharist are, of course, the best visual aids of all. They have been given to us by Jesus himself and carry a powerful message, which he has promised will bear fruit. But they are not only visual; they also involve us by touch and taking part. They do not achieve anything different from the word of the Gospel, but they do appeal to us through different senses – not only hearing but also seeing, touching, tasting, receiving. They are 'visible words'. But the words must be included, if the sacraments are to be interpreted in a way which makes sense to the participants. This creates a problem with the practice of some churches which have instituted 'communion by extension' so that lay people can take bread and wine – which has been consecrated by a priest in a church service – and use it in another service where no priest is available. In this case, they do not use the words of thanksgiving or Jesus' words of institution because the priest has already said them. But the words are for the benefit of the worshippers, not for the benefit of the bread and wine! The words are essential if the sacrament is to have any meaning for the participants. Without the words, the sacrament is at best meaningless and at worst a magic charm.

The two gospel sacraments of baptism and Eucharist are rich in symbolism. They make use of the most basic necessities of life – water, and the food and drink on the table. It is more important for the Church to use both ministers and elements which are locally available than to bring in special celebrants and buy in special wine and unleavened wafers. Ordinary, everyday commodities are made by Jesus to speak to us of God's love and his mighty acts of redemption. They do not just enter our minds but touch us and make a difference. Both of them focus primarily on Jesus and his death on the cross. They are an embodiment of Paul's driving passion – 'to know nothing among you except Jesus Christ, and him crucified' (1 Corinthians 2.2). They portray and confirm what is already well known, but are also evangelistic visual aids. They do more than explain the good news; they demonstrate it.

In the New Testament those who heard about Jesus, and believed, at once received the sacrament of baptism to assure them of the reality of God's grace. Of course they would need teaching in order to ensure they understood the gospel – but this teaching would normally follow baptism; it was not a condition or a qualification for being baptized (as has often been the case in the modern Church). The only qualification was the response of faith. Believers would then see and feel that they were united with Christ in his death and resurrection as they went down into the water to be cleansed and rose again as new men and women in Christ. So today preachers should make sure that they not only explain but also *show* this symbolism by means of the action of going down *into* the water and coming *out* again. Sprinkling drops of water does not achieve this. Full immersion may not be necessary, but even babies can be dipped into water and taken out again. Baptism symbolizes not only cleansing but also a funeral (the end of the old life without God) and new birth (life with Jesus).

In the Eucharist the elements used should be as near as possible to ordinary food and drink – although some say that we should use unleavened bread and wine as Jesus did, even though we may not normally have these on our tables. Bread and wine should, ideally, be separate – not mixed – to symbolize the shedding of blood in death. Also ideally, one cup and one loaf should be used to symbolize the oneness of the family of God in Christ (1 Corinthians 10.17) – though some today feel unhappy about sharing one cup because of the danger of infectious diseases. The 'taking', the 'thanking', the 'breaking' (of the bread) and the 'giving' of the elements should be done as visibly as possible in the sight of everyone. In this way the sacrament is truly a visual aid which supports and confirms the preacher's message. That is how Paul put it to practical use in 1 Corinthians 10 and 11.

Special Note C
AN AFRICAN STORY

The Pair of Shoes

Translated and adapted by Wendy Bowen from a Tanzanian traditional tale in the collection made by Daudi Muhando, 1962.

Between the forest and the river there was a very lonely village. Here lived a small boy called Tano. One day Tano's uncle came to visit, and he gave Tano a mango. Tano had never before tasted anything quite so sweet.

'Well, if you like it so much, why don't you plant the stone and grow your very own mango tree?' said his uncle.

So Tano planted the stone carefully by the river bank. The stone sent down roots into the damp earth and grew slowly at first, but by the time Tano was grown up, the tree was many times taller than he was. For ages it only had dark-green, glossy leaves, but then one year it had a huge crop of red and green mangoes. Tano gave away as many as he could, but he still had basketfuls left over.

'What shall I do?' asked Tano. 'The mangoes will go bad before we can eat them.'

'You will have to take them to market,' said the wise old men.

'What is a market?' asked Tano, who had never been out of his village except to catch fish from a boat on the river.

'It is a place some miles away along the path by the river bank,' said the wise old men. 'There you can exchange your mangoes for something else.'

'But what if I get lost?' replied Tano.

The wise old men laughed. 'You can't possibly get lost. Just follow the path by the river all the way until you come to a town. The people there will tell you what to do.'

So Tano put the mangoes in a large basket and set off with it carefully balanced on his head. After walking for about three hours, he reached the town as the wise men had said. Immediately he was surrounded by a big crowd who all wanted to buy his mangoes. In exchange they gave him coins which they explained were called 'money'.

When the basket was empty, Tano had time to look around him. He noticed that everyone else seemed to have strange pieces of leather on their feet which they called 'shoes'. Tano had always walked about barefoot. So when he saw a man who had many pairs of shoes piled up before him, he asked all about them.

70

'Shoes stop your feet from getting wet or cut by stones or prickled by thorns,' said the man.

'How wonderful!' said Tano. 'Could I have some shoes of my own?'

'How much money have you got?' asked the man, and when he saw the coins which Tano held in his hand, he exchanged them for a fine pair of brand new leather shoes.

Tano put them on and started to run back home along the path, very pleased with himself. Not only were they shiny and bright; they also squeaked as he walked, 'Eeek! Eeek!' Then he thought he could hear someone laughing.

'Someone is laughing at my shoes!' he thought and, looking up into a tree, he saw a monkey.

'I'll teach that monkey to laugh at me!' He looked round for a stone to throw at the monkey. But he could not find anything. The only thing to hand was his shoes, so he took one off and threw it at the monkey to knock him down out of the tree.

But the monkey caught the shoe instead, and ran off with it into the forest, chattering loudly as he went. The chattering grew fainter and fainter until Tano was left standing alone in the silence, with one shoe on and one shoe off.

'Never mind,' thought Tano, 'I still have one shoe,' and he tried to walk home – but, as everyone knows, it is not easy to walk with one shoe off and one shoe on. After a while, he stood still and took off the other shoe.

'It's no good,' he said. 'I'll have to take this back to the market and get my money back.'

He ran back as fast as his bare feet could carry him. Luckily the shoe-seller was still there.

'I don't want this shoe,' he panted, all out of breath. 'Can I have my money back?'

'Where is the other shoe?' asked the shoe-seller. 'We only sell shoes in pairs. One shoe on its own is worth nothing.'

Poor Tano! He went round all the market stalls, and however much he reduced the price, no one would give him anything for his shoe. In despair threw his one useless shoe after the other one, and walked home with no shoes, no mangoes and no money. But back in the village, the wise men turned his adventure into a lesson for all the children to learn. One shoe they called *What I say*, and they called the other *What I do*. These two things must always go together. One without the other is useless.

A story like this can be applied to people's lives in several ways, e.g. Faith *and* Action *belong together; or at a baptism show the relationship between what I promise and what I do; or show the relationship between the historical Jesus who lived and died 2,000 years ago and his Spirit who lives in us now. In every case it shows that one is useless without the other. They belong together. Children can easily act out a story like this.*

Special Note D
RITES OF PASSAGE

*I preach because the Church is there and I preach that the Church might be there.
Church preaches to Church.*

Dietrich Bonhoeffer

Rites of passage is the name given to the big events in the human cycle
of life, especially involving families: birth; initiation (when a child becomes an adult); marriage; death. Preachers have a special part to play
on these occasions. More often than not, they will be speaking not so
much *to* the congregation as *for* the congregation – as its mouthpiece
(see p. 45). In one sense, this is another place where visual aids are involved, but this time the visual aids are not manufactured but embodied
in the people and in their life stories. These are the basic raw materials
for the preacher to use, even more basic than the Scriptures (see below).
Sometimes, it is just the church liturgy which is involved. But sometimes we need to link with traditional customs which originated in the
community long before the Church took root there.

Birth

At the outset, we must recognize the distinction between celebrating
the birth of a baby and baptizing a baby. Those who hold firmly to
'believers' baptism' do not have a problem here, but paedobaptists
(those who baptize infants) are often tempted to treat baptism as if it
were a rite of passage. It is not; it is a gospel sacrament, to be admin-
istered only within the household of faith. To give thanks to God,
however, for the wonderful gift of a new human life is a ceremony in
which all should be involved, whatever their faith. Special rituals for
this already exist in some cultures. Whether they do or not, the Church
should want to be involved – and perhaps take the initiative in offering
the family its own ceremony as a suitable way of saying 'Thank you'.
Many churches have special liturgies for this purpose, and there will
be an opportunity for a short sermon to say what the family feels and
wants to express. The God who gives new life is the same God who has
revealed himself in Christ and in the Scriptures – and the preacher's
task is to make clear the links between them, i.e. between nature and
grace.

Initiation

This is such an important ceremony in many cultures, marking the passage from childhood to adulthood, that the Church cannot afford to ignore it. Long ago in 1913 Bishop Lucas, taking the advice of his Tanganyikan colleagues, saw that the churches were failing to meet this need which the people felt so strongly. So he introduced the Christian *jando* (for boys) and *malango* (for girls), which combined African and Christian symbols in a new way (Anderson, 1977:99–101). Christian preachers and teachers were involved, along with the traditional teachers, giving guidance about responsibilities and morality in adult life. But this was in the early days of the Church in Tanzania. Today the Church is strong enough to ignore the customs of traditional society – but it will be wise not to do so. The transition to adulthood should still be marked by suitable ceremonies and courses of teaching (rather than a lot of sermons!).

Marriage

The most important requirement for the preacher is to establish a close relationship with and understanding of the couple who are to be married, and probably of their family too. (The same applies to funerals.) Spending time with the family beforehand enables them to trust the preacher. Trust is essential if we are to minister effectively in such intimate situations. Otherwise the excitement (or grief) of the moment will prevent anyone from listening to the words spoken. This does not mean that you cease to expound the word of God. It is just that you start where they are, i.e. with themselves. They are the raw material for your sermon. Then, having aroused their attention to the relevance of what you are saying, move gently to the application of the word of God to their situation. There are many different ways of doing this.

One way is to use the element of surprise. The late Bishop Festo Kivengere (Coomes 1990:239), a particularly imaginative speaker, was preaching at a marriage when the young couple were surprised to hear him taking as his text Exodus 25.20, which describes how Moses is to make two golden cherubim to 'face each other' and to look 'towards the mercy-seat'. Festo told the couple that they should always face one another, but focus their eyes and attention on the Lord Jesus, our mercy-seat, 'where all failures and sins are forgiven. That's where you will learn to forgive and encourage each another.'

Sometimes we are required to conduct weddings of people who don't know much about the Christian faith and are not much interested in the Bible. In such cases, the preacher must find out what they are interested in, and use that to unfold before them the meaning of God's love.

The *Harry Potter* series of books has become popular with adults as well as children. They have been made into films and translated into many languages. They tell the story of a schoolboy at Hogwarts, a boarding-school for wizards. It is not in any way a Christian book but, at its heart, repeated in every volume, is a tale of self-sacrificing love – i.e. just what weddings are supposed to be about. When Harry was a baby, the Evil One, Lord Voldemort, killed his father, then tried to kill Harry, but his mother intervened, crying, 'Don't kill him; kill me instead.' She was duly killed, but when Voldemort turned to Harry, he found that he had no power to harm anyone who was loved with so great a love. The one thing which the Evil One cannot understand is love. So Harry was an orphan who never knew his parents – but he loved them and treasured their memory. So far from abandoning him, they had died for him (Rowling, 1997:216)! This is the foundation not merely of marriage, but of human life – not how much we love, but *how much we are loved* – this is what gives us security and confidence and leads the preacher naturally into John 3.16, 1 John 4.10 and many other gospel texts.

Death

Preachers cannot afford to be lazy about preaching at weddings or funerals. People soon realize if you have not bothered to understand their lives. On such occasions, preachers must do more listening than talking, and show that they are emotionally involved with the people. A wedding packed with guests at Nairobi Cathedral one Saturday had been carefully planned for months and was an occasion of great gladness – but only four days later the very same people were back in the very same place for something they had never planned, and the mood was quite different. After the wedding, one of the cars carrying four guests had gone off the escarpment road, and now it was the day of their funeral. The preacher had to show the people that his mood matched theirs. It is good if preachers can show that they too are emotionally affected by sorrow, for this gives permission for others to cry.

The famed Nigerian writer, Ben Okri, has written of his 'appalling experience' when his mother died:

> What can I turn to? The religious structures, the Church, helped, but not as deeply as I thought it would. This is a terrible thing to say. The reason is because at the time I experienced something very peculiar. I realized that the pastor who was speaking to me about grief, spoke to me from a

book but not from experience, so he could not speak to the grief in me. He could not speak to the emptiness in me because, at the time, he hadn't gone through it himself . . . About four years later his own mother died and he wrote to me and said: 'Oh my goodness, I didn't know. That's what you were going through at the time.' (2004:28)

But preachers must do more than understand. They must also show that in the midst of sorrow they have good news, which can bring confidence out of despair. Here too, we must start where the people are. The shape of the sermon should arise out of the time we have spent with them beforehand, feeling their pain and putting the service together. If all their thoughts are about their departed loved one, so must ours be – but they must not stay there. A funeral service should be about the dead, but for the benefit of the living. Some of them can't believe it has really happened; others will feel angry, others guilty. Preachers have to understand the stages of grief, discern the emotions, echo them on behalf of the people, and then, so far as possible, help them to move on – but without offering instant solutions. To understand is more important than to provide answers. They may need permission to be angry (as writers in the Bible sometimes were); they will certainly need an opportunity to say 'Sorry' – to the deceased, and to one another – and to imagine the deceased wanting both to forgive them and also to share in the penitence. (The new Church of England funeral liturgy has a place for this to happen.)

The *Harry Potter* books contain a good example of this. An old couple had reached the astonishing age of 650 years, by the power which resided in 'the philosopher's stone'. But this stone also had much evil influence, and it was Harry's mission to destroy it. He was deeply upset that his action would lead to their death. Professor Dumbledore reassures him, 'Do not think, Harry, that the death of this old couple will be a tragedy. Death, after all, is the start of a new adventure' (Rowling, 1997:215).

Funeral sermons should be short and simple, using one or two memorable phrases which can stay in people's minds afterwards. They must try to say what is true – but also what is kind and encouraging at a time when people are vulnerable. If the deceased person is known to have lived a bad life, you cannot suddenly praise her as if somehow death has made her good. But you can imagine she may have had good intentions, and offer a sure hope in God's mercy. A common Bible reading at funerals is John 14.1–6. People often ask for it because it seems to offer a comforting answer to the question 'Where is she now?' But it doesn't really. It actually offers something much more profound – the possibility of a new start for the living. Thomas' question was a logical one which anyone would ask – 'Tell us where you are going; then we can understand the way to get there.' Every human journey begins by deciding first where you are going, then working out the way. But Jesus tells his disciples that for them it will be the other way round. Stop worrying about the destination; just get your feet on the way and stay close to me. Then your troubled hearts will be at peace, for I am the Way. The only sure way to get close to the departed loved one is to get close to Jesus, who has gone ahead. He is the key to reunion with the ancestors, for he alone knows them and us thoroughly.

When a young Christian mother died in East Africa, there was inconsolable grief, as young women led the cries of mourning. Two young pastors came to sit with the family, supporting them in their distress, and began to sing quiet choruses of praise to Jesus the Redeemer. Gradually others joined in, and the sense of victory in Jesus began to overcome the despair. Grief was never forbidden, never banished, but when it came to the sermon, all was quiet and good news overcame the grief with hope and triumph.

Special Note E
THE DEVELOPMENT OF
PREACHING IN EUROPE
David L. Edwards

Once in seven years I burn all my sermons, for it is a shame if I cannot write better sermons now than I did seven years ago.
quoted by John Wesley, *Journal*, 1 September 1778

For last year's words belong to last year's language
And next year's words await another voice.
T. S. Eliot, 'Little Gidding'

The missionary movement led preachers all over the world to copy the styles of preaching developed in the Western world since the Enlightenment of the eighteenth and nineteenth centuries. This meant that preaching tended to be an analytical, reasoned presentation of Christian truth, appealing primarily to the minds of the hearers. This, however, has not always been the style of preaching in Western churches. Different styles have featured in various eras. The Very Revd Dr David Edwards outlines the historical developments of preaching in the West. This is a shortened version of his article in the Church Times *on 25 October 2002.*

Styles of preaching evolved continually over the years in the churches in Europe. Many parish priests were not educated enough to do anything more than say a few simple words in explanation of the day's Scripture reading, or comment on people's behaviour.

But the orders of friars who used to travel about the villages were skilled at presenting both logical teaching and the great stories of the Bible vividly – and often humorously, adding stories of miracles or conversions – to arouse people's enthusiasm to follow Jesus. They often used the pictures in the stained-glass windows, or carved in stone, to illustrate their words. The great Franciscan preacher, St Bernardino of Siena, wrote,

> If of two things you can only do one – either hear the Mass or hear the sermon – you should let the Mass go rather than the sermon . . . there is less peril for your soul in not hearing the Mass than in not hearing the sermon. (Smyth, 1940:15, 16)

A few very well-educated clergy were able to preach eloquently, often in Latin. But after the Reformation, when the Bible was available in ordinary English, people wanted preachers to explain it to them clearly. Not many preachers were able to do this (there were no training colleges), so the Church provided homilies, which were approved for reading out in parish churches; or catechisms, which taught people by the question-and-answer method.

But a big change came with the Puritans in the seventeenth century. They did not want to impress people with their learning or to entertain them, but only to save them and get them to know and love the Bible as their guide for living. Preachers used to meet together in classes to help one another in their sermon preparation. Every sermon ended with remarks on the 'use' of the text, i.e. how it applies to your life today and tomorrow.

After 1660, English sermons became fashionable and elegant, carefully reasoned but not inspirational, until the evangelicals of the eighteenth century revived the Bible-based preaching of the Puritans, passionately urging people to be 'born again'. They wrote hymns on biblical themes, so congregations could together sing their response to the word of God. Sermons were thus integrated into the whole service, which was enjoyable, relevant and drew large congregations. These evangelicals gave birth to the missionary movement, which wanted to bring to the whole world the good news of Jesus as they understood it.

During the nineteenth century, the 'catholic' movement arose in the Church of England, and preachers began to give systematic instruction about 'what the Church teaches' rather than 'what the Bible says'. Soon afterwards, church-going became less fashionable in Europe in the light of the growth of the new sciences and higher criticism of the Bible. However, both evangelical preaching and catholic teaching remained alive and well in the new churches being planted in Africa, Asia and Latin America.

In Europe, faith seemed to be dying rather than growing, so preachers found themselves trying to defend the Bible by answering the questions of its critics, e.g. is there a loving God? Is there life after death? How much of the Bible, or of the story of Jesus, can we believe? Is its ethical teaching relevant today? Many sermons in Europe today still try to deal with these questions. But people's deep desire is for spiritual life for themselves and for justice in society – so preachers are now asking, 'How can we meet this need from the word of God?'

Because of new forms of communication like TV, people in Europe are now thinking more in images than in long, linear arguments. They are used to short 'sound bites'. They concentrate for just a few minutes at a time. They respond to pictures, songs, drama – which is just what church services are capable of providing but have often failed to do. The new challenges are being met in some of the following ways:

1 'Services' may happen on weekdays as much as on Sundays, in homes or clubs as much as in church, for cell groups as much as for congregations. But whatever form they take, somehow the message must be communicated.

2 Not only the parish priest, but also lay believers should be ready to lead in worship, to bear witness to their own experience of God's love, and to share their reflections on a Bible text. The simpler and less 'expert' this is, the more authentic and powerful it may be.

3 'Sermons' can take the form of sound bites of just two or three minutes each – perhaps one thought on a text, a song or even on a real-life experience. A variety of voices will be welcome. Nowadays, not only in Europe, preachers can expect to find well-educated experts in their congregation, who can help to throw light on a variety of topics.

4 The use of drama or videos can stimulate both preachers and hearers to engage with matters which are relevant to contemporary life. Whatever the topic, it should relate to daily life and so what is presented in the pulpit ought to be discussed with the congregation. Let them ask questions, make contributions, and even answer back! Sometimes this discussion can take place before the sermon, in which case the people will realize that they have shared in formulating the message – it is partly their sermon!

5 What happens at meetings of church leaders? Do they just discuss money, or problems of the parish or diocese? Why not adopt the Lutheran example of discussing the Bible passages set in the lectionary for the following Sunday? See pp. 116–17.

6 Some will wish at times to have longer, more serious forms of instruction, similar to the traditional – or even Puritan – type of sermon of 30 minutes or longer. This can include debate. Space must always be made for this to happen – perhaps by gathering the young people, or the professionals, or the leaders in a group of local churches, and then using the services of visiting, qualified teachers to conduct teaching and sharing sessions.

Study Suggestions

1 What lessons for the congregation could you draw out of each of the two stories on p. 53 and out of the story on pp. 70–71?

2 In 2 Samuel 12, Nathan told King David a story with an unwelcome message (see p. 21). What methods might a modern preacher use to say to important and powerful people things which they do not want to hear? See also pp. 127–9.

3 What legends, if any, does your culture have which link up with the world of the Bible or with the world of today?

4 How does Exodus 18.13–27 show the importance of the ministry of lay people? What sort of people, in your experience, are most ready to take part in public ministry? What sort of people would the congregation most like to hear from in an interview?

5 What posters have been used by Christians in your country or in your church? What message does each one convey? How effective are they? Evaluate any film you have seen, e.g. the *Jesus* film or *The Passion of the Christ*.

6 What actions were used in the passages mentioned on p. 63 section 2, and what message did they convey? What other symbolic actions can you recall from the Bible?

7 What features of local interest do you know of, which could illustrate a sermon?

8 If you watch TV, think of two or three common human problems you have seen portrayed there in dramatic form. How could you relate these to the life of your congregation?

9 How effective as symbols of the gospel are the sacraments of baptism and the Eucharist as practised in your church? Pick out the elements which speak clearly to people.

10 In your country, what concerns are uppermost in people's minds at times of marriage, and of death? Suggest ways in which the preacher can address their needs.

11 What books, or films, or interests are generally popular in your country? Can you use these as contact points in sermons on Sunday, or at marriages or funerals?

12 Write your own funeral service. What message do you hope the preacher might give to those who mourn your passing?

13 Consider how preaching developed and changed in Europe (Special Note E). Which of those sorts of preaching, if any, would best communicate in your culture today? Which of the suggestions 1 to 6 (p. 80) might be helpful in your local church?

5

RHETORICAL SKILLS

God calleth preaching folly; do not grudge to pick out treasures from an earthen pot; the worst speaks something good.

George Herbert

Politicians need to win votes and gain supporters. To help them do this, they learn the skills of persuading people by means of effective speaking. This skill is called 'rhetoric' or 'oratory'. Political leaders employ professional speechwriters, who do not need to know much about politics or economics but do need to know popular culture, great literature (e.g. the Bible) and how to use words (see Atkinson, 1984, to which this chapter owes much).

Preachers do not expect people to applaud their sermons, but they do hope – and pray – that people will respond to Jesus and follow him faithfully. On rare occasions a preacher may aim to change whole societies, as Martin Luther King Jr did in opposing racist policies in the USA, or Desmond Tutu and Allan Boesak in opposing apartheid in South Africa. Huge crowds hung on their words which gave oppressed people new hope – it was not surprising that in these circumstances the audiences responded loudly.

Preachers can learn rhetorical skills from people like this and from politicians, as they try to make people think, to touch their emotions and to lead them to action. First of all, preachers should not speak *at* the people but *identify with* them, i.e. use 'we' rather than 'you'. Anyone who has a vision of God's purposes for his people needs to show that the message is first for the preacher, and then for everyone. Using such skills will often make a sermon memorable – but that is not our aim: our aim is to move people to change and to act. Often speakers should look for dramatic ways of saying something which will grab people's attention instead of saying the same thing in basic language which is easily forgettable. Some examples are given below.

1 *Lists of three*

> The obvious example is 'The Father, the Son and the Holy Spirit'. The Bible has others, e.g. 'Jesus Christ, the same yesterday, today and for ever'.

'Government of the people, by the people, for the people'
  – Abraham Lincoln (instead of saying simply 'democracy').
'*Ein Volk, ein Reich, ein Fuhrer*' – Adolf Hitler (instead of saying the
  German equivalent of 'the German people are united in one
  nation-state under one leader').
'We are a party united in purpose, strategy and resolve'
  – Margaret Thatcher.

Two-part lists are too short but five-part lists are too long (though
this may not always be true). Audiences may not realize it, but they
are used to hearing lists of three. So the speaker should say the first
two parts of the list with a rising intonation of voice, and the last
one with a falling intonation. This shows that the three belong
together, and that now the picture is complete – even though the
speaker may go on to say more about each one of the three parts.

This is not the same as trying to construct a sermon with three
points, as preachers are often taught to do. Kivengere found that it
was not wise for him, as an African, to aim at a 'carefully balanced
three-point structure', partly because that was not his way of thinking and partly because the message (or the text) should determine
the shape of the structure, rather than a predetermined shape being
allowed to control the message.

2 *Contrasts*

'To be, or not to be; that is the question' – Shakespeare's *Hamlet*.
'Man is born free, and is everywhere in chains' – Rousseau.
'Ask not what your country can do for you, but what you can do
  for your country' – President John F. Kennedy.
'We shall have to learn again to be one nation, or one day we shall
  be no nation' – Margaret Thatcher.
'That's one small step for man, one giant leap for mankind'
  – Neil Armstrong, the first man to walk on the moon.

3 *A puzzle*

By 'a puzzle', I mean a phrase which people have to think hard
about to realize what it means.

'And now I would ask you a strange question: who is the most
  diligent bishop in all England; that passes all the rest in doing his
  work?' said Bishop Latimer in 1548. This really made people pay
  attention and think, but he went on to give a long and vivid
  description of Satan, who was always busy deceiving people and
  especially church leaders.
'This is not the end; it is not even the beginning of the end; but it
  is perhaps the end of the beginning' – Winston Churchill.

'Never in the field of human conflict has so much been owed by so many to so few' – Winston Churchill (instead of saying, 'The air force has done Britain the greatest possible service').

4 *'Set them up and knock them down'*

The speaker begins by saying something the people agree with to make them feel comfortable, then turns it into a sharp challenge. The Bible has many examples, e.g.

- The story of injustice which Nathan told King David (see p. 21).
- A love song about a vineyard, sung at an agricultural festival, led up to denouncing Israel's injustice (Isaiah 5.7).
- Amos (1.3—2.8) criticized the crimes of the nations, then turned to denounce Judah and Israel for their injustices.

A Zulu pastor preached a sermon to a backsliding congregation. He began with a humorous story to make them listen and laugh. Then he suddenly applied the story to them – they gasped and were convinced (Sundkler, 1960:166).

5 *A repeated refrain*

Amos 1.3—2.8 is a good example of this; see also the speeches of Martin Luther King Jr and Allan Boesak, below, and the sermon by Dr Gitari (pp. 127–8).

6 *A suitable quotation (maybe in a foreign language)*

'Two thousand years ago the proudest boast was *Civis Romanus sum*; today in the world of freedom the proudest boast is *Ich bin ein Berliner*' – President John F. Kennedy, visiting Berlin, 1963 . . . but the quotation must be both simple and familiar to the people.

A Kenyan preacher, when a new president took office, began by rejoicing that Kenya had never had such godly leadership, but then warned of the challenges we might face under three 'bishops', i.e. Askofu Biblia, Askofu Taifa and Askofu Siasa. Everyone tried to guess who he was thinking of, but he showed that these were pictures from history – Amos (the word of God), the Emperor Constantine (the state) and Karl Marx (political revolution). Each had good features, but there were dangers also.

See also the speeches of Churchill and King, below.

Sometimes a proverb can be quoted in its original language – but you may then need to translate it (or invite the congregation to do so) for those who do not know that language.

7 *Alliteration*

This is when there are several points in a sermon, each beginning with the same letter – or even having similar endings, e.g. Information, Inspiration, Intercession.

'Bermondsey is more important than burgundy; council houses
than country houses; comprehensive schools than colleges' – an
English politician saying that the needs of ordinary people are
a higher priority than the comforts of the rich and privileged.
Or, on leadership: 'What a good leader needs is the indignation
of hindsight, the illumination of insight and the imagination of
foresight' – Bishop David Pytches (note also three points).

Alliteration can be helpful to people, but should be used sparingly,
and be true to the message. As in all sermons, the form must never
control the content.

8 *Anachronism*

This means describing something in terms of a different period of
time. Preachers can make the Bible come alive today by portraying
a biblical incident as if it were an event in the twenty-first century,
e.g.

- Naaman (2 Kings 5) could be 'Field-Marshal Al-Hajj Naaman,
  who was HIV-positive (v. 1), drove in his Mercedes with a fleet
  of lorries (v. 5) and motor-cycle outriders (v. 9) to Elisha's mud
  hut, only to see the house-servant Gehazi shuffling out in his
  carpet slippers, telling him to wash in a muddy ditch (v. 10)'.
- Or you could imagine people getting news of something by
  reading the church press (Acts 11.1) or by finding a copy of the
  Jerusalem Echo (Acts 8.28).
- Zacchaeus (Luke 19) could be interviewed by a roving TV reporter, who finds furniture vans lined up outside his big house
  and Zacchaeus saying,

  > It's all got to go, furniture, books, carpets – the lot. Hospitals, Old
  > People's Homes, Schools, that sort of thing . . . Jesus Davidson came
  > and sat at my table and gave me love. It wasn't God in church any
  > more, expensive and out of reach; it was God in my house, making
  > Himself like me, trusting me. (Jackman 1960:77)

Kivengere, in one of his sermons, made Zacchaeus look like the
local receiver of revenue, 'and there was the tax department of
Nairobi before us in living colour', commented one listener. 'Is that
the same story I read in my Bible?' (Coomes, 1990:389).

This is similar to what Bible translators do when they translate
the *meaning* of a word rather than the literal word itself, e.g. 'The
Lamb of God' for the Inuit people (who have never seen sheep)
becomes 'The Baby Seal of God' in order to communicate with
them effectively. Preachers should be doing this all the time, and
there are many ways of doing it. One way is by making vivid links

between the message and the actual people, places or events which are familiar to all of us here in this place, today. Sermons which fail to do this may faithfully expound the word of God (which should be our primary aim) but just sound like a piece of ancient history.

9 *Afterthought*

It is possible Jesus sometimes added a sentence as an afterthought to his parables which would have a lasting effect on the hearers. One obvious example can be found in John 8.7 – 'Let anyone among you who is without sin be the first to throw a stone at her.' It was certainly an effective final remark.

A barrister called Edward Marshall Hall was once defending a poor prostitute who had been unjustly accused of murder. After he had finished summing up his case to the jury (who were to decide whether or not she was guilty), he sat down – but immediately stood up again, pointed to the woman and challenged them, 'Look at her, gentlemen, look at her. Life never gave her a chance; won't you?' The verdict was 'Not guilty'.

10 *Pause*

Clearly in 9, above, the speakers made good use of a pause. We can learn a lot about 'timing' of this nature if we listen carefully to professional actors and comedians. Pauses should be used quite often. If a major point has been made, a challenge issued or a question asked, it will help the listeners if they are given a few moments to digest what has been said before having to listen to the next point. Preachers must always be thinking how the listeners are likely to respond in their minds to what has been said. In some places – e.g. in Africa, in black churches in USA or in inner-city congregations in the UK – people will shout out if you ask them a question. But others will think that it is their place to sit quietly in church and just listen obediently to the preacher, however little they understand or like it! In that case, you can ask them what they really think – and then give them time to think, or even to discuss it with their neighbour. On many topics, the thoughts of the people may actually be more reliable than those of the preacher – and wise is the preacher who recognizes this. Pauses show that you do. Martin Luther King Jr, in his 'dream' speech, below, paused not before his phrase, 'I have a dream' (as you would expect), but after it, each time. The pause made the phrase belong to the preceding sentence, and drew emotional responses from the crowd. It was an odd place to pause, but it worked.

11 *Gestures*

It is important to use your eyes, hands and facial expressions to convey your meaning. There are no rules about this – you will need a listener to tell you if, for example, you are making the same gesture repeatedly, and probably meaninglessly. If you are using sermon notes, you can add emphasis to a point by leaning forward and making eye-contact with the congregation. If you wear spectacles, take them off sometimes, or use them in a gesture. You do not need always to hide your notes – you can use them in gestures, as Winston Churchill often did.

Four speeches are reproduced below as examples of many of these stylistic features which help to make the message more effective. The Study Suggestions will help you to analyse these features and reflect on how they are used.

Winston Churchill, 1938

I will begin by saying the most unpopular and unwelcome thing: that we have suffered a total and unmitigated defeat. The utmost that my Right Honourable Friend the Prime Minister has been able to secure by all his immense exertions at Munich and elsewhere (*interruptions*) . . . the most that he has been able to gain for Czechoslovakia is that the German dictator

> instead of snatching his victuals from the table
> has been content to have them served to him
> course by course.

For you will find in a matter of months that Czechoslovakia will be engulfed by the Nazi regime. Her frontier fortresses are already in German hands – something which France and Britain will bitterly regret when Herr Hitler chooses to look westward.

> Silent, mournful,
> abandoned, broken,

Czechoslovakia recedes into the darkness. That is the most grievous result of what we have left undone for the last five years;

> five years of looking for the line of least resistance,
> five years of uninterrupted retreat,
> five years of neglect of our air defences.

> The British people should know
> that we have suffered a defeat
> without a war,
> that we have passed an awful milestone in our history when the
> whole equilibrium of Europe has been deranged, and

that these terrible words have been pronounced
against the Western democracies;
'Thou art weighed in the balances and found wanting'.

And don't suppose this is the end.
This is only the beginning of the reckoning.

This is only the first sip, the first foretaste
of a bitter cup which will be proffered to us
year by year . . .

Unless . . .

unless, by a supreme recovery of martial vigour,
we arise again and take our stand for freedom!

Martin Luther King, 1963

*Dr King's speeches were repeatedly interrupted by the huge crowd with exclama-
tions and applause. He was identifying with the people and speaking not so
much to them, as for them. Only a sample of these interruptions is given below.*

I have a dream
that one day on the red hills of Georgia, sons of former slaves and sons
of former slave owners will be able to sit down together at the table
of brotherhood.
I have a dream
that even the state of Mississippi – a state sweltering with the heat of
oppression, sweltering with the heat of injustice (*Yeah! Yeah!*) – will
be transformed into an oasis of freedom and justice (*Amen, Amen*).
I have a dream
that my four little children (*Amen! Yeah! Yeah!*) will one day be able to
live in a nation where they are not judged by the colour of their skin
but by the content of their character (*applause, Amen! Amen!*).
I have a dream.

I have a dream
that one day little black boys and little black girls will be able to join
hands with little white boys and little white girls as sisters and
brothers.
I have a dream today.
. . . This will be the day when all God's children will be able to sing
with new meaning,
My country, 'tis of thee

Sweet land of liberty
Of thee I sing.

Land where my fathers died,
Land of the pilgrim's pride,
From every mountainside
Let freedom ring!

And if America is to become a great nation, this must become true.
So let freedom ring!
From the prodigious hills of New Hampshire let freedom ring!
From the mighty mountains of New York let freedom ring!
From the heightening Alleghenies of Pennsylvania let freedom ring!
From the snow-capped rockies of Colorado let freedom ring!
From the curvaceous slopes of California . . .
But not only that: let freedom ring from Stone Mountain of Georgia;
Let freedom ring from Lookout Mountain of Tennessee;
Let freedom ring from every hill and molehill of Mississippi;
From every mountainside let freedom ring!

And when this happens, when we allow freedom to ring, when we
let it ring from every village and every hamlet, from every state and
every city, we will be able to speed up that day when all God's
children – black men and white men, Jews and Gentiles, Protestants
and Catholics – will be able to join hands in the words of that old
Negro spiritual:

Free at last,
Free at last,
Thank God Almighty
We're free at last!

Martin Luther King, 1968

. . . and he's allowed me to go up to the mountain top (*Go ahead!*)
and I've looked over (*Yeah!*)
and I've seen the promised land. (*Holy! Holy! Amen!*)
I may not get there with you,
but I want you to know tonight that we as a people
will get to the promised land.
So I'm happy tonight.
I'm not worried.
I'm not fearing any man –
mine eyes have seen the glory of the coming of the Lord!
                              (*The next day, Dr King was shot dead.*)

89

Allan Boesak, 1990

We see the tears on the cheeks of those who have buried loved ones
who have died in the struggle, and we share their grief,
and we know the price is high, but the end is near.

We see at this moment justice still stumbling on the streets of South
Africa, and apartheid still reigning on the throne of this land,
and we know the price is high, but the end is near.

We hear the voices of the beast as it shouts at us, as it tries to frighten
us, as it tries to intimidate us,
and we know the price is high, but the end is near.

We know, we know that we will have to pay, and it is costly, and the
struggle is long and hard, and the road is arduous;
the price is high, but the end is near.

Do not despair, do not look around, do not betray our faith, do not
betray our children, do not betray our fathers, do not betray our
mothers, do not betray our vision, do not betray the justice we are
fighting for, do not betray the land we will see, that will rise up out
of the ashes of this country, as apartheid will crumble to dust.
The price will be high, but the end is near.

Hear me, le Grange, hear me, P. W. Botha; hear me also, O my
people. Leave this church today strengthened and strong and faithful
and clear in your own minds.
The price is high, but the end is near.

The Dangers of Rhetoric

The purpose of including the above quotations is that they contain
many stylistic features which preachers can use effectively at any time,
provided they do so only occasionally. However, most of these speeches
were delivered to large crowds at times of danger or challenge. It was
necessary for the speakers to stir the emotions and wills of the people
by using a declamatory (formal, oratorical) style, which would not be
appropriate for the normal Sunday sermon in an ordinary local church.
It would normally be unwise to fill one's sermon with such strong
rhetoric. A conversational style would be more effective. Style depends
partly on the nature of the message and partly on the number of people
present. Another obvious danger is that listeners will admire the preacher
so much that they will never get the message about following Jesus in
obedient discipleship. Watching Dr King's speech on TV, President
Kennedy exclaimed, 'Magnificent!' and the BBC reporter said that
Dr Boesak spoke with the voice of angels. For this reason, many gifted
speakers have made a conscious decision to simplify their style when

preaching and to give up using rhetorical skills – so that Jesus may be seen, not the preacher (see the quotation from Baxter on p. 50).

In any case, the New Testament, unlike the Qur'an and much of the Old Testament, was not written in a beautiful literary style or in a sacred language but in *koine* Greek – the language of the street and the marketplace – and our preaching should reflect not only the content but also the forms which Jesus and the apostles used (see p. 102).

There is also a theological reason for not relying too much on rhetorical skill. This is based on 1 Corinthians 1.18—2.5. Even though he knew that the citizens of Corinth admired rhetoric, Paul refused to use this skill because he also knew that the effectiveness of Christian preaching comes from the power of God's message, not on the skill of the preacher to persuade (or even brainwash!) the hearer (Thiselton, 2000:107f.). Paul's 'word of the cross' not only says something. Like the word of the Lord through the prophets, it also *does* something – it creates faith in those who hear it, and changes them (Romans 1.16; 1 Corinthians 2.4, 5). The popular newspaper, *The Times* of London, runs a competition to find the 'best' sermons of the year. But this is a misplaced exercise. It forgets that true sermons belong to one time and one place and cannot be effective outside the setting for which they were prepared. And you cannot truly assess the merits of a Christian sermon unless you were in that place. In the words of Leander Keck: 'Paul saw (in 1 Cor. 1.28, 29; 4.20; 2 Cor. 4.7) that you can't justify the preacher or the message by the norms of the culture without surrendering the message of the cross' (Keck, 1978:53). Those who seek credit for good performance end up either proclaiming themselves or offering 'another Jesus'. The extracts given in this chapter were speeches rather than sermons, aimed at political action for justice rather than spiritual commitment to Christ.

St Augustine compared the skills of preaching with the skills of rhetoric. Preachers, he wrote, should first pray that God gives the message. Second, they should make the quality of the content and the welfare of the hearers more important than the outward form. Third, their words should be clearly understood. But he recognized that sermons should be not only instructive but also enjoyable to listen to.

Special Note F
WOMEN'S WAYS OF PREACHING
Esther Mombo

Truth can never be told so as to be understood and not be believed.

William Blake

Most of the preachers in the history of the Church have been men. Some Christians think Jesus intended it that way, but many disagree. There have always been women preachers, but now in most churches it is common to hear women preaching. Many people have asked whether there is any difference between the way men and women preach. Here are some answers to that question which have been suggested:

1 *Women are more aware of new challenges to the dominant culture, and are better at witnessing to them (like the women at the empty tomb and at the incarnation); men tend to affirm the dominant culture.*
2 *Women often reflect their experience in vulnerable ways; men like to expound the text.*
3 *Women weave various threads together and leave untidy ends; men like to tie up the ends.*
4 *Women 'connect' with the realities of life; men sometimes think in abstract principles.*

However, all these are dangerous generalizations which may not prove true in particular cases, especially when we try to apply them to people of different cultures. Dr Mombo, Academic Dean at St Paul's United Theological College, Limuru, Kenya, reflects on this.

It is hard to say what makes preaching different for women. I would want to avoid suggesting that all women are somehow by nature different from men when they preach. However, I think that women who are aware of where they have come from in the Church (that only a generation ago there were no women preaching) do approach the task differently. This is to say that women who are aware of their place in the story of the Church would preach differently in the contexts in which they find themselves.

The preacher is a detective of divinity who goes out into the world, looking for God's extraordinary presence in the midst of the mundane (a God she is able to recognise through the lens of the Scriptures), she then goes into the pulpit while she is still shaking and trembling with the wonder of the discovery, offering to share that treasure she has found with others. (Taylor, 1993:15)

The above fits in well with what I would consider women's ways of preaching. In this short reflection I wish to talk about the type of women who preach, the context in which they preach and the methods they employ to preach. To begin with, it has been argued, and rightly so, that women form the majority of church members in Africa, and it could be true in other parts of the world. Most women preachers are lay, especially in rural parts of Africa. Some are pastors, theological students, teachers and leaders of women's organizations. In most places women will preach in women's groups, in others in mixed services.

The context of women's preaching varies from one place to another. In some places it is acceptable for women to preach; in others it is unacceptable. The reasons for this include the culture of a particular group of people, or the way the Bible is interpreted, or in some cases the doctrine of the role of women as defined in a particular church. Most women's preaching takes place in an atmosphere of not being accepted. Preaching by women is not an issue for God but for people. Some people are not sympathetic to the cause of women because the sermons they hear are usually preached by men. Some male preachers use examples of women as sinners, tempters, seducers who lead men to fall into sin. Such sermons fail to encourage men to be responsible for their sins but stereotype women as sinners and dangerous. Male preachers tend to pick stories that disempower women and continue to subordinate them. The more men preach, the less women will hear about the good news that liberates all of us.

Against this background we look at the methods employed by women preachers:

1 Most women will be 'teacher-preachers', which involves a 'call-and-response' approach. The preacher involves the congregation in some form of dialogue. The congregation is made to think and laugh and see themselves and also God more clearly.

2 Most women use their experience in preaching. In doing this, they affirm their right as distinctive beings to resist being treated as objects and being defined by others. They have the power to define their own realities, and it gives them a stronger position in society, increasing their sense of value as persons who have much to contribute to the whole.

3 African women theologians use cultural hermeneutics (interpretation) in reading Scripture. These women argue that the interpretation of

Scripture has to take seriously the role of culture in dealing with issues that affect society, and particularly women.

4 Story-telling is a significant method of preaching, especially by women, in areas where the Bible is largely told as a story rather than read, because of high levels of illiteracy. This method also has advantages because of the nature of stories in Africa.

> A substantial body of African stories are gender neutral. Stories do not always feature men and women or girls and boys. Instead, they might feature animals whose biological gender is not specified. The story thus manages, to some degree, to pass wisdom and values indiscriminately to its listeners. African stories also carry 'flat' characters, e.g. the hare in South and East Africa, or the spider in West Africa, which represent values and philosophies of survival. (Dube, 2001:3)

Story-telling as a method of preaching lessens the problem of language and gender stereotyping. A story in this case can be used to warn, to send a disciplinary message, to instil morality or to affirm people. This method is significant in the African Instituted Churches, most of which were founded by women. When they preach they invoke the same Spirit who came upon the women of old. This helps to explain why they are preachers and leaders. It is a way of confronting patriarchal churches and societies which have denied them opportunities to preach. Although many stories in the Scriptures are negative towards women, these preachers capitalize on the stories which are liberating to all.

5 Women use a social analysis or prophetic method of preaching. They engage with issues and situations of struggle for social justice, including gender justice. Most women preachers will name the issues or expose the deceptive forces in our world that seek to imprison and oppress. These forces take the form of systems, powerful people, language and ideologies which are death-producing for us. At other times, these forces are internalized and people are trapped by their own thinking, deceived into denying their own value as human beings. I have to add that men, especially church leaders in Kenya, have also used this method. They have been good at confronting powers that affect them, but I would argue they have not concerned themselves with gender issues, especially those which affect women.

6 The use of metaphor is central in women's preaching, including things like voice, story, actions, etc. Each metaphor is an integral part of the human experience of emotions, thought, speech and actions. It is a way of knowing that expands our understanding of reality, and enables us to see something new by referring to something familiar. Women's preaching does not need to imitate male preaching or

screaming male voices, but rather to opt for imaginative ways of presenting the word of God to change people's lives for the better.

The struggle for women is not to be like men in preaching, even if their training takes place under patriarchal (male-dominated) norms. Women who preach should not have to seek to be accepted, but do need to think critically about their preaching, the stories they use, their actions, voices, themes and how they characterize women in their sermons. The sermons should be designed to challenge people to move well beyond the limitations that have been placed on them in the past. They can do so by listening more intently to the voice of God and learning to trust their own voices.

> Preaching is liberation. We speak to set people free . . . There can be no redemption of the self without a liberation of the social world, and no redemption of the social world without release from the self's inner bondage. All we are saying is that preaching, as it shares God's saving purpose, will be a liberating word. (Buttrick, 1994)

When preaching leads to the community's expression of vision and hope, it has announced good news.

Study Suggestions

1 Name any public speakers you have heard whose rhetorical skills have impressed you, whether or not you agree with what they say. Try to analyse what makes them effective.

2 What three other rhetorical devices, apart from 'puzzle', do you notice in the two quotations from Churchill on pp. 83–4?

3 (a) In each example given on p. 84, what are the words of the refrain?
   (b) What device did Dr King use in 1963 (p. 89) which was similar to that used by Amos?

4 Sometimes a foreign word, or phrase, is used in the Bible (e.g. the Egyptian word used in Genesis 41.43). Can you think of any others? What effect do you think it has on the reader?

5 How did Dr King and Dr Boesak make links between their message and the concrete situation confronting the people at that time?

6 Read the four speeches on pp. 87–90 several times and identify or underline all the rhetorical devices used by the speakers. Imagine the effect this way of speaking had on those who were listening.

7 Can you think of any other rhetorical devices which you have heard speakers using? In what situations, if any, might such devices help you to get your message across?

8 Why should there be a contrast between the skill of a sermon and the power of the gospel? See 1 Corinthians 1.18—2.5. What advice about preaching would you give to an experienced public speaker who was about to be ordained pastor?

9 What do Christians in your locality think about women preaching as much as men do? What reasons do they give for welcoming the preaching of women – or for resisting it? What is your own opinion?

10 Make a list of ways in which you think men and women might differ from one another in the way they preach. If possible, support your opinions from your experience of listening or of preaching. If you are a man, compare your answers with those given by a woman; if you are a woman, compare yours with a man's.

6

INTERPRETING AND USING THE BIBLE

Preaching is thirty minutes in which to raise the dead.
John Ruskin

There are three principal types of preaching, according to J. W. Z. Kurewa (2000:90): doctrinal, topical and biblical. *Doctrinal preaching* focuses on the beliefs and doctrines of the Church, and can be an effective way of instilling basic teaching into people's minds and also of doing basic evangelism. A doctrinal sermon may use a text or a credal statement but may appeal to many biblical texts to support the picture of, say, who Jesus is, what the Holy Spirit does, the nature of a human being, the nature of sin or the atonement. *Topical preaching* may take a contemporary issue of general concern, e.g. corruption in public life, marital faithfulness, war and peace, tribalism, homosexuality, etc. This method was often used in Africa to point out the need for liberation from colonial rulers. It is likely to take a current viewpoint as its starting point but then to appeal to the Bible to support the message. This book shares the view of Kurewa that by far the best type of preaching is *expository, biblical preaching*. This is the form of preaching with which the remainder of this chapter is concerned.

Students of the Bible are usually taught in college that it is necessary to understand the language of the biblical text, its historical and cultural background and its literary form. Finally, having understood the text, they must ask how it fits with their systematic theology. They are usually taught that this practice is useful for both student and preacher. Here are some examples.

Language

It is helpful to know Greek or Hebrew, but whether preachers know these languages or not, they ought to use commentaries which can explain the language of the text. For example:

- *Mark 1.41* says that Jesus was 'moved with pity', but an important manuscript says 'moved with anger'. If Jesus feels angry about all that spoils human life, then this text gives us material for a powerful sermon.

- *Deuteronomy 15.5, 9, 10* is about cancelling debts every seventh year. The words used are 'obey, open your hand, lend, give', but the Hebrew uses a rare construction which says, 'Obey-obey, lend-lend, give-give.' This gives special emphasis to the obligation to cancel debts. Society normally says, 'Debtors must *pay* their debts', but Moses insists that 'Creditors must *cancel* debts'. The preacher needs to reflect this special emphasis, e.g. 'Really obey; really give.'

History

Texts make the best sense if we know the historical situation of speaker and audience:

- *Isaiah 55.1–3*: The Jews were in despair under the domination of Babylonian rule. Exiled and exploited, they struggled for the basic necessities of life. But God's word offered them freely the best food and drink – in other words, a new life of freedom in covenant relationship with their generous God. 'Imagine it; things don't have to be like this; another life is possible.' God gives hope to the hopeless.
- *Matthew 2.1–12*: A preacher may expound this text paying much attention to what happened – what was the star and how did they follow it? But too much attention to this aspect of the 'history' will prevent people from seeing the point of the story or the writer's intention. Matthew saw in this story a vivid picture of his own church situation where most Jews had rejected their 'king' but Gentiles were flocking to worship him.

Culture

Some – but not all – Bible language refers to customs or culture which are unfamiliar to readers today. For example:

- *Romans 3.24*: 'Redemption' means setting someone free by the payment of a price. This was the experience of slaves in Roman times or, perhaps, in Africa in the nineteenth century – but it needs to be explained, perhaps by telling the story of how a real person, Roman or African, was set free.
- *Galatians 2.15–21*: 'Justification' is notoriously hard to explain – but perhaps a story of a judge in a court of law can bring the theology to life for today.
- *John 1.29*: 'Lamb of God' is easy for a Jew to understand – but not for an Inuit living in the Arctic (see p. 85), nor for most of today's city-dwellers, who will need some help.

Systematic Theology

Most mature Christians know what they believe, and when they come across teaching in the Bible or the Church which seems to conflict with this, they naturally try to interpret it in a way that fits in with what they believe. It is not wrong to do this (see p. 23), but it can create problems. For example:

- *James 2.24* seems to conflict directly with Paul's teaching about being justified not by works but by faith (Galatians 2.16 etc.). Preachers may worry about this, but should examine carefully James's situation and argument. Was it different from Paul's? Do people not need to hear James's own message for them, without Paul being allowed to 'correct' it?
- *John 8.11*: Jesus rarely condemned anyone except self-righteous, religious leaders. He was more concerned to save and restore them. These days many liberal Christians say that homosexuality is perfectly all right in God's sight, as long as there is real love and nobody is getting hurt. Evangelical Christians reply that the Bible condemns it – yet they may easily fall into the opposite error (which Jesus never did) of just criticizing and condemning people instead of loving them as they are.

It is all too easy to read our own bias (i.e. our own presuppositions) into every text, especially those which we find difficult, uncomfortable or challenging. The danger of this is that we can prevent the Bible from saying anything to us which we have not already thought. In this respect Martin Luther is an example of both good and bad practice. As a monk, he had understood the words 'the righteousness of God' (Romans 1.17) to mean God's justice in punishing sinners – but one day he saw that it really meant the good news of how God 'justifies' believers, i.e. makes them right in his sight. Luther wrote,

> I felt myself to be reborn and to have gone through open doors into paradise. The whole of Scripture took on a new meaning and whereas before the 'justice of God' had filled me with hate, now it became to me inexpressibly sweet. (Bainton, 1955:49, 50)

At this time he was ready for the Bible to surprise and change him. But later on he had problems with other parts of the Bible. He called the Letter of James 'a letter of straw', and when he commented on Galatians he kept thinking he could see references to the Pope (of whom Paul could have known nothing). In other words, later in life he saw all his own thoughts reflected in the Bible. Even today many evangelicals read the writings of Paul through the spectacles of Augustine or Luther, and so assume that Paul's conversion saved him from his sense of guilt before God (as had been the experience of Augustine and Luther) – whereas Paul said in Philippians 3.4–6 that he did not feel guilty, but that on the Damascus road he heard God 'calling' him to proclaim that Jesus is the promised Messiah. Similarly, some Christians interpret words about salvation and the kingdom of God in terms of social justice, and others find their own views about capitalism or communism supported from the Bible. But they run the risk of reading *into* the Bible ideas which are not there and fail to read *out of* it the ideas which are.

The writers in the Bible were not writing systematic theology. They were different people who reflected different perspectives of God's truth. No preacher could ever fully explain, for example, the atonement to his hearers in one sermon. But we could vividly explain how one person saw it on one occasion. The Bible usually tells us 'the big story' by means of a lot of smaller stories about ordinary people who are not heroes of faith. This connects with the listeners, who feel themselves to be more like a Naaman who needs healing or a nervously witnessing serving-maid (2 Kings 5.3), than like the wonder-working Elisha. As a young Kenyan said after reading Mark's Gospel for the first time, 'I felt it was all about me.' Our own stories take on meaning when they find their place in the larger story of which God is the author (Wilder, 1964:78).

Preachers who are not ready to accept new truths from the Bible will be tedious to listen to because every passage will seem to contain the same message. There will be no variations or surprises. If they continue to read their own views into the Bible, then the Bible will never be able to reform and change them. But those who read the Bible through the spectacles of the original writers will find not just their own ideas there, but new vision and new guidance.

One way of correcting our biases is by writing down the main themes of our Christian thinking, and then testing our sermons to ensure that they do not always reflect just our own ideas. We could ask ourselves: What do I understand God to be like? or Christ? Is the incarnation or the cross or the resurrection most central in my thinking? How do I regard sin? What is the main thing in salvation? Is the Christian life a triumph or a struggle? Is my spirituality centred on the Church or my home or society? Is the mind or emotions or actions most important for me? Do I learn from traditional teaching or from experience? Finally, do I allow my reading of the Bible to challenge me in all these areas?

Those who preach for the first time, having studied all these matters, often try to use this knowledge in order to inform their congregations of the content of the text, i.e. what it means. In the Western world, preachers have often asked themselves, 'What is the big idea in this text?' and then constructed a three-point sermon which is long enough to give necessary information but short enough to retain the interest of the hearers. But such sermons often sound rather like college lectures, which deal effectively with the world of the text but do not connect with the world of today in which the hearers live. The hearers may find that such sermons are like boring or irrelevant essays, even though they may be expertly prepared and delivered. But we must take account not only of the *content* of the text but also its *style* or *form*, as we tried to do in Chapter 5 – the contents of the revelation are inseparable from the forms in which they are conveyed. We shall now attempt to do this in relation to three different sorts of literature which we find in the Bible: letters, stories and prayers. But first we must note one very important feature of the New Testament.

Speech and Writing

Most of us are used to reading books, and we do so silently. But in the early centuries of the Christian era, people could not read unless they did so aloud. St Augustine was astonished to discover Ambrose, Bishop of Rome, reading a book without making a sound! And certainly the books of the New Testament were read not so much *by* people as *to* people. The Gospels record an oral tradition of what Jesus said and did, and the Letters were read out loud to their recipients (Colossians 4.16). When we preach from the Bible, we are putting the typescript back into the form in which its writers wanted to communicate it. The word of God is not static but dynamic, and it needs the preacher to make it so. Martin Luther was therefore quite correct to write,

> . . . the proclamation should take place by word of mouth, publicly in an animated tone [see Gal. 3.1; 4.20], and should bring that forward into speech and hearing which before was hidden in the letters . . . Christ Himself did not write His own teaching as Moses did his, but gave it forth by word of mouth and commanded that it should be done orally. (Quoted in Wilder, 1964:23f.)

This is reflected in very many cultures of the world, where people do not read or write their own vernacular languages very fluently – but these are the languages in which they think and feel. They probably use a second or third language – French, Spanish or English – for writing, but it is the vernaculars which touch the heart. Some well-educated Tanzanian pastors write their sermon notes in English as I do, but preach in Swahili or in their own vernacular, for English is the medium of writing but the local language is the medium of meaning and emotion.

The Letters of the New Testament
(see Day, 1997:273ff.)

Writers of New Testament Letters used many different styles to communicate with their readers. We can use these different styles to bring the message to life for today. This is what the incarnation means in practice for the preacher. Just as God was embodied in human flesh, so preachers have to take the form of the message as seriously as its content. For example:

1 *The situation*

The New Testament Letters were written to real people about the situations they were facing, the questions they were asking or the mistakes they were making. The only way to understand the message of each is to understand the different circumstances of their readers (see the example of James 2.24, on p. 99). Jesus said to one group of people, 'Whoever is not with me is against me', and to another, 'Whoever is not against you is for you'. Texts are not static statements, so preachers need to recapture the dynamic situations to make sense. By doing so they will find they connect with the real situations of their hearers today. Even the Letter to the Romans may seem like a statement of systematic theology, but Paul was actually in his workshop hammering out his thoughts bit by bit in the face of the problems which were facing both him and his readers. The details (e.g. Jews versus Gentiles) of the problems are not the same as ours, but often the problems themselves are similar. When preachers find it difficult to express wonderful and complex truths, they should not pretend to their hearers that it is all really rather simple, but invite them into their workshop to join in the struggle together.

2 *Personal feelings*

The Letters bring us close to the writers. We hear Paul longing to be with his readers (Galatians 4.20; Romans 1.11) – for different reasons. He pleads with them (2 Corinthians 10.1); he appeals to their reason (Romans 6.3); he rebukes them (Galatians 3.1); he even shares with them his deepest experiences (2 Corinthians 12.1–10). Preachers need the courage and honesty to do the same, and to reflect not merely the content but the mood of the New Testament. Why not tell the congregation how much you thank God for them, and pray for them? Paul did, and added, 'Please don't let me down' (Colossians 4.17; Philippians 4.9). It has been suggested (p. 111) that women preachers may find it easier than men to do this.

3 *Poetry*

Some of the most profound passages in Paul's letters are pure poetry (see Philippians 2.5–11; Colossians 1.15–20) – but often we try to explain them by turning them into prose, and so miss the power of the original. Perhaps we need not only to accurately analyse the content but also to be captivated by the poetry and reflect it in the style of our preaching. And if Paul's letters sometimes quoted familiar songs or sayings (Ephesians 3.14), should we not be ready to do the same?

4 *Controversy*

When we overhear Paul's impassioned debates with his opponents (e.g. the diatribe in Romans 3.1–9) we should not remain calm and detached but join in – so much so that we get our hearers involved as well! They certainly will get involved if we translate the details of the tension between the 'weak' and the 'strong' in Romans 14 into the tensions which our churches are facing today. Such a style lends itself to dramatic presentation in church, with different people taking the parts of the different protagonists in the debate.

5 *Autobiography*

This feature is found frequently in Paul's writings and also in Peter's and the Pastoral Epistles. It is not always easy to translate this across the centuries which separate us from the New Testament, but this is how Fred Craddock preached on 'You have heard, no doubt, of my earlier life in Judaism. I was violently persecuting the church of God' (Galatians 1.13):

> Then imagine how the young Saul feels. Generations and generations of being the people of God and now someone in the name of Jesus of Nazareth gets this strange opinion that it doesn't matter any more, that Jews and Gentiles are alike. You must sense how Saul feels. All your family and national traditions, all that you have ever known and believed, now erased completely from the board? Every moment in school, every belief held dear, every job towards which your life is pointed, now meaningless? Everything that grandfather and father and now you believed, gone? Of course, he resolves to stop it. The dark cloud of his brooding bitterness forms a tornado funnel over that small church, and he strikes it, seeking to end it. In the name of his fathers, in the name of his country, in the name of God, yes. (Day 1997:281, quoting from Lowry, 1989)

Put like this, it resonates not just with Saul's situation but with countless others today!

This is real preaching, even though it may have fallen out of use in some cultures. It takes the Bible seriously as the word of God, not just for what it says, but for how it says it. It enters into the dynamics of the real situation, linking with real personalities and telling real stories.

People will listen and respond, just as they respond to any of the great stories of the world.

The Stories of the Bible
(see Goldingay 1984:261ff.)

Just as it is good to use the different styles found in the Letters in our preaching, we should do the same when we preach on stories. Often, however, the preacher gives a summary of the story and then tells the congregation what it is all about under three or four headings. To do this is to rob the story of its power because we have abandoned the story form – which is the form in which God does most of his communicating with us! It is better to retell the story and then reflect on it, perhaps by replacing the ancient idioms with modern ones which mirror people's actual experiences today (see p. 85), then tell more of the story, and reflect, then more, etc. This is how we talk to children – but you can be sure that all adults pay great attention to any good children's story, well told! Alternatively, we can tell a different story, either traditional or modern, which throws light on the Bible story not because it says anything different but because it says the same thing in a new and unfamiliar way (see pp. 53–5).

Stories do four things:

1 They paint a picture of a situation, usually focusing on some problem or difficulty. Listeners may need help in understanding its background if the story comes from a different culture. The preacher should do this by making brief, vivid comments rather than describing the culture.
2 Stories show how people tried to solve the problem and failed. At this point the listener begins to identify with the person in the story – 'He's just like me . . .' – especially when modern idioms are used. The 'Ignatian' imaginative method is one effective way of doing this (see p. 59).
3 Stories show what went wrong and how the difficulty was overcome in the end.
4 They may finish off by telling the listeners how there can be a happy outcome in their own lives too, either through their own efforts or with the help of others. But more often the lessons are so obvious that the story can be left to speak for itself – anyone can see how it applies to them.

The whole of the Old Testament is really an epic story of the people of God, starting with the creation. But this one story includes many short stories which are self-contained. The books of Ruth, Jonah and Esther are good examples, but so is the long story of Joseph and the six short stories about Daniel. Similarly the New Testament has four central histories of the life, death and risen life of God's Messiah; but within these are many short stories, of which some are histories of what Jesus did and others are fables which he told. All stories have something to say to later readers, like us – as Hebrews 11 shows very clearly.

This book has already referred to commonly told folk-tales (see p. 52). Usually these carry a moral lesson for the reader: 'So this is how you should behave . . .' Sometimes moral lessons of this kind are to be found in the stories of the Bible, but more often the Bible tells us stories which indicate not what we should do but what God has done and is doing and will do, for us and in us. In other words, they are in the indicative, not the imperative, mood (see p. 24). The Bible contains lots of examples of God's people behaving in questionable ways (e.g. Genesis 12 and 22), but of how God fulfils his purposes for good through, or often in spite of, the actions of human beings.

The stories of Jesus' miracles are slightly different. They have been called 'the trailing clouds of his glory which he brought from heaven with him'. In other words, they are just what you would expect if Jesus was who he claimed to be. They give a picture of who he is, rather than of what his followers can expect in their daily life. The 'signs' in John's Gospel make this particularly clear (2.11; 12.9–11), as does the ending of the Gospel (20.31). These, like those recounted in the Old Testament, are the events on which our faith rests. Israel did not succeed but failed, repeatedly; the stories show that it is their God who was faithful. Some Christians, however, claim that these stories are intended to guide us in our actions today. Liberation theologians justify their action for justice for the oppressed poor on the grounds of God's actions to deliver his oppressed people from Egypt in the Exodus; and many Pentecostal Christians claim that deliverance from sickness in the name of Jesus is the God-given right of all believers (see p. 63). The stories and images in the book of Revelation are so difficult to understand and to preach on that Calvin would not attempt to write a commentary on it. However, there have been times when this book was the most used in the whole Bible; for example, by Lisu Christians who were persecuted and exiled from China in the 1950s, or by Rhodesian Christians – white and black – at the time of the liberation war.

Stories create a world before our eyes. That world is in many ways similar to our own, but is arranged into a meaningful pattern, which makes us 'see' that a different world is possible. In that world, the poor and hopeless are rescued and made 'kings and priests'; or a woman's life falls apart but is remade through the loyalty of a foreign refugee; or a prophet runs away from God, is called back by some pagan sailors, preaches reluctantly to the heathen, and then is angry with God when they repent and join him in the faith; or a country preacher is executed but returns to be with his followers for ever; or a bunch of ignorant peasants turn the world upside down by telling people about this preacher. Life would be easier without these stories – but also poorer and duller. They draw us into their world, but also make us afraid of it – maybe because God is in it, maybe because it's too good to be true. Preachers must tell and retell these stories, for 'the real world in which God invites us to live is not the one made available by the rulers of this age', who promise us so much and give us so little. Preachers offer 'an evangelical world . . . shaped by the news of the gospel . . . still longingly received by those who live at the edge of despair, resignation and conformity' (Brueggemann, quoted in Goldingay, 1997:93).

The New Testament book which is pure story, without much explanation, is Mark. He lets the story of Jesus just speak for itself. Preachers should at times be silent, and just let Jesus speak, through his own story.

A Note on Parables

Some stories in the Bible are presented as factual, others are pure fiction – and it is not always easy to know which is which. To ask, 'Is it true?' may sometimes be an irrelevant question. Some of the 'history' does not always seem very edifying. But Jesus' parables, obviously fictional, are as 'true' as anything we have ever heard – provided that we really *can* hear them. The Prodigal Son is a powerful story but, like other stories, we have to be sure that it makes sense in terms of the culture of its hearers. For example, not many English people would realize that when the younger son asks his father for his inheritance now, what he really means is, 'Dad, I wish you were dead.' Nor would they understand how unthinkable it would be for a respected father to *run* to meet his son – it would be an intolerable loss of face. And a better title for it would be 'The Two Lost Sons'.

The Revd Joe Kapolyo of Zambia explains that this story would need some reinterpretation for the Bemba people, because their society is matrilineal (based on kinship with the female line). A man inherits his estate from his mother's brother (his uncle), on the uncle's death. The uncle marries his third wife, whom his nephew also desires. The nephew comforts himself by thinking, 'When my uncle dies, I will inherit her.' But the uncle does not die, the nephew's desire grows insatiable, and he persuades the woman to sleep with him. It is the equivalent of telling his uncle, 'I wish you were dead!' When a Bemba woman heard this version, she leaped up and shouted, 'That can't happen; it's outrageous!' – just as Jesus' hearers would have reacted to his story. She would have listened quietly and politely to the story of the Prodigal Son because it does not relate to her world. So we may need to alter stories a bit in order to get an equivalent reaction from the audience.

The essential feature of Jesus' parables is that they taught people about the new world, called the kingdom of God, by means of pictures from this world. As Jesus described it, the new world did not come across as something fantastic and unreal but as a real possibility of the present world being redeemed and transfigured. We can be saved just where we are! If we want to do what Jesus did, we cannot simply repeat the images he used, for they do not belong to the world in which our hearers live today, and to use them would falsify his message.

Preachers must first understand the ancient forms and the meanings which they conveyed. Then, instead of 'demythologizing' them or turning them into dry prose, we must imitate those ancient writers and, by the use of our imagination, create new images which speak to our world of today (see Wilder, 1964:126ff.). We need to ask, 'What in my world corresponds to a peasant farmer patiently waiting for seed to grow, or to a slave being redeemed from bond-service? Who is today's equivalent of a good shepherd, or of a father killing the fatted calf?' The questions are endless, and the answers we give will be different, depending on our local culture – not only racial or geographical, but rural or urban, agricultural or nomadic. We are challenged to be as creative as the writers of the New Testament, so that communication leads not merely to understanding but to belief and commitment. The first Christians created credal statements in order to express their faith using the cultural forms of their time and to counter the heresies of that time. We have inherited these and still repeat them in church today – but if we were truly creative, we would perhaps find different forms and different words to speak to our different world. One who matched those early writers in creativity was John Bunyan, the author of *Pilgrim's Progress*, and in recent times Festo Kivengere and Martin Luther King Jr have been equally creative in their use of oral word-pictures.

The parable of the Rich Fool is all about the question of inheritance and land. These are emotional issues in most societies. Jesus refused to adjudicate about who was right and who was wrong in this question (Luke 12.13). He introduced a new perspective altogether. This is what Kenneth Bailey (1983:73ff.) tries to do in a way which would be relevant for the lives of people who live in Palestine today, all the time worrying and fighting over land. He calls his poem 'Ode on a burning tank' because it starts by describing the spilling of blood, the burning of army vehicles and the misery of violent, unmourned death. Then the poem continues – and it is really a vivid picture of reconciliation.

. . .

The voice told this ancient story;
Precious blood intoned this ancient tale.

A certain man had two sons.
One was rich, the other was poor.
  The rich son had no children
  while the poor son was blessed with many sons and many daughters.

In time the father fell ill.
  He was sure he would not live through the week
  so on Saturday he called his sons to his side
    and gave each of them half of the land of their inheritance.
    Then he died.

Before sundown the sons buried their father with respect
  as custom requires.

That night the rich son could not sleep.
  He said to himself,
    'What my father did was not just.
    I am rich, my brother is poor.
    I have bread enough and to spare,
      while my brother's children eat one day
      and trust God for the next.
I must move the landmark which our father has set in the middle of
the land so that my brother will have the greater share.
    Ah – but he must not see me.
    If he sees me he will be shamed.
    I must arise early in the morning before it is dawn and move the
    landmark!'
With this he fell asleep
  and his sleep was secure and peaceful.

Meanwhile, the poor brother could not sleep.
  As he lay restless on his bed he said to himself,
    'What my father did was not just.
    Here I am, surrounded by the joy of many sons
      and many daughters,
    while my brother daily faces the shame
      of having no sons to carry on his name
        and no daughters to comfort him in his old age.
    He should have the land of our fathers.
      Perhaps this will in part compensate him
      for his indescribable poverty.
  Ah – but if I give it to him he will be shamed.

I must awake early in the morning before it is dawn
and move the landmark which our father has set!'
With this he went to sleep
and his sleep was secure and peaceful.

On the first day of the week –
very early in the morning,
a long time before it was day,
the two brothers met at the ancient landmarker.
They fell with tears into each other's arms.
And on that spot was built the city of Jerusalem.

The Two Horizons

Perhaps the chief point made in this Guide is the need to 'translate' the ancient text into the language of today. Theologians have described this process as recognizing 'the two horizons'. This is possible first because God has given his Spirit to help us to understand the Bible, and second because we share the humanity and the faith of the people in the Bible, and their experiences throw light on ours and open up new possibilities for our lives.

Any reader will assume that the story of the Good Samaritan is simply telling us to be kind to those in need. But it is not. Its real message is that the very people you most despise and hate can even show you how you should live your life. This means you should not only be kind to such people but also be ready to receive the blessings they can give you. All Samaritans were despised by the lawyer to whom Jesus was talking. 'Priests are good; Samaritans are bad,' he thought. By making a Samaritan the hero of the story, Jesus was deliberately turning his world upside down. But this picture of a Samaritan means nothing to people today. The preacher has to paint an equally vivid picture but change the characters, in order to communicate the meaning.

The process involves two main steps. The first is understanding the language and culture of the writer of the original text, so that we know exactly what he wanted to say. This has been called 'decoding'. We have to do this before we ever consider how the text might meet the needs of people here and now. And we must also recognize what our own assumptions might be – we may need to correct them if we are to uncover the real meaning of the text. For example, most Christians assume that Pharisees were bad people because Jesus had so many arguments with them. But this is not what the Jews of that time thought, and we must first think like they thought if we are to interpret Jesus' story of the Pharisee and the tax-collector correctly.

The second step is harder still. You may have discovered a message within the original text, but you must then understand the language and culture of the people to whom you minister, and translate the biblical text into that culture. Imagine doing this in the case of the parable of the Good Samaritan. You may have to tell your listeners, as Jesus did, to admire and even to imitate the actions of people whom both they and you hate or despise. It will be difficult for you to say and difficult for them to hear. It will feel like a betrayal of all that is most dear to them. Kenneth Bailey, who lived in the Near East, wrote, 'I can only confess that in twenty years I have not had the courage to tell a story to the Palestinians about a noble Israeli, nor a story about the noble Turk to the Armenians' (Bailey, 1983:48). Miroslav Wolf (1996:9) of Croatia described facing the same struggle when he was challenged to embrace a Serbian fighter. Almost all the stories which Jesus told 2,000 years ago must be told differently if they are to bring the same message to us today as they brought then. Preachers must ask themselves how they will say today what the Bible said thousands of years ago, without altering its meaning in the process.

This applies to other parts of the Bible too. When we read 'Jesus is Lord' (1 Corinthians 12.3; 2 Corinthians 4.5), we must recall that this was the baptismal confession which every Christian made at their baptism. It meant different things for different people. Jews regarded it as blasphemous because it used for Jesus the same name as they used for Yahweh. Gentiles would interpret it in terms of a slave being at the disposal of his master, or of a pagan worshipper being devoted to his god. It would not be right to understand it in the light of Roman emperor-worship, because emperors did not demand worship until after the time of Paul. For Paul himself it would remind him of the commission he received on the Damascus road to take the message of Christ everywhere. Preachers must work on making one or more of these meanings relevant to their hearers today.

Prayer Texts
(see Goldingay, 1984:270ff.)

Writers of the Epistles speak to *us*; in stories people speak to *one another*; but the writers of the psalms are speaking to *God* – but we can overhear what they say and enter into their experiences and emotions. We often do this when reading Hosea or Jeremiah or Paul, but the book of Psalms gives us a unique example of this type of writing. This means that we can preach on it in a unique way.

It could be appropriate, instead of explaining the meaning of the words, to let the feelings of the writer be shared by preacher and congregation.

As we listen, we can echo the words and the emotions – in praising, confessing, giving thanks, asking, complaining, weeping, or even being triumphant. We can do this in short snatches and, in between, use short periods of silence to allow ourselves space to feel what the psalmist feels – and to realize that this is how we really do feel, even though the details of our circumstances may be different. We may also discover feelings which we never realized we had. We have suppressed them, but hearing them voiced by the psalmist uncovers them (just as when you get married you discover things not just about your partner but also about yourself!). But the psalms don't just help us to recognize the nature and authenticity of our feelings. Their ultimate aim is that our relationship with God should develop and grow in maturity. If we can admit to feeling, at different times, hurt, anger, despair and guilt, then we shall gradually become open to receiving God's response. This response may not comfort us in the way we hoped, but it may lead us to meet him and praise him for his care of us. A sermon which uncovers who people really are (in relation to God) is probably more useful than one which tells us exactly what to do.

The question for preachers is whether they can show their emotions in public in the way the psalmist does, and then listen to the experiences and emotions of others. It all involves a level of sharing which we often try to protect ourselves from. Are women better at this than men, as Sharon Kyle has suggested (1997:260), or are people of one culture better at it than those of another? This process of sharing feelings may help us to see aspects of the biblical revelation which we had never noticed before. A Westerner may know Jesus as 'my personal Saviour' but may not have noticed the importance of belonging to one another in his community. An Israeli knows all about his rights to the land, but may forget his obligations to strangers who live there. A rich person may need a poor person to show her that Christians should be concerned about politics as well as faith. A city-dweller may need help from rural friends to see the significance of Psalm 72. Entering into the world of the psalmist brings us face to face with the psalmist's God. The psalmist speaks for me; and his God speaks to me – and both messages may be new for me and lead me into new experiences of God.

Reviewing the Process

Those who are newly ordained as pastors or commissioned as lay preachers might well worry about how to interpret the Bible correctly in their preaching. As students they probably studied the Bible critically, from a distance, but they must now come back to it as God's word to them today. They should ask, 'How can I use the little I have learned to bring the word to life as I preach?' But in fact it is not so difficult, and we do not need to become expert Bible scholars in order to preach good sermons. Remember: a good sermon is one people listen to, and they will always listen if we relate our words meaningfully to their world. That is why the late Bishop Festo Kivengere used many memorable slogans – 'because I have something to say, and I ask myself, how am I going to say it in a way which will help people listen?' (Coomes, 1990:436). Theological study ought to help us in our preaching, but Festo found that it did not always do so. 'I was losing my freshness', he wrote. So he decided, 'I must be careful not to lose my understanding of the African way of communicating. I made up my mind that Western influence should help to clarify my thoughts, but not force me into a set mould' (Coomes, 1990:240).

Instead of worrying about textual, historical and literary criticism, we should spend more time praying that God will show us what the writer meant to say to his hearers in the text, and how that message can come alive for our hearers today. New Testament writers did just that. They discovered in their Bible – the Hebrew Scriptures – a message that gave people new hope and turned the world upside down. Our world, so full of hopelessness, can rediscover that hope if preachers come to the biblical text and ask it the right questions.

So, to summarize much of what has been written above, those who are called to preach should take the following essential steps in order to interpret the texts before them:

1 *Pray*

We are called to hear the word of God as it was spoken, or enacted, in the past, and to expect it to bring God's message to us for today. We must ask the Holy Spirit to give us understanding – and to make us responsive and obedient. This is not the only time to pray about our sermon. The whole process should be surrounded by prayer, not only by the preacher, but by the congregation also. Finally, it is important to create at least ten minutes of quiet to pray before the service begins, and then have time for a brief prayer before actually starting to preach.

2 *Listen*

Although preachers are called to speak, their first task is to listen. There have been many preachers in the history of God's people to whom God did not speak – yet they prophesied; they were not sent – yet they went. See Jeremiah 23.21. We listen both to the text and to today's context (p. 16), which has been called 'double listening'. This second listening may occur as soon as we turn to the text, but more often during the longer process of meditating upon it – see below.

One of the problems in listening is that we know the Bible quite well – so well, in fact, that it no longer surprises us. Dr Elsa Tamez, of Costa Rica, thinks it is important to gain distance from the text, especially from those texts which are most familiar to us (Sugirtharajah, 1991:54). Read it as if it is new and you are seeing it for the first time. Let the text suggest new words and pictures to you. Then, as Bishop Kivengere found, it will be new for the hearers also. This requires a conscious effort, and perhaps reading it in a version, or a language, different from the one you usually use. When we have 'gained distance', then we can 'come closer' again to the text by bringing to it our own daily life experience of pain, joy, struggle, celebration, etc. A storm on the lake (Luke 8.22) will make us think of crises which suddenly burst into our lives. Women can read it as women without interpreting it through a man's way of thinking and will bring fresh insights to images of childbirth (Romans 8.22) or child-care (Hosea 11.3, 4).

3 *Meditate*

Listening leads to meditating. We begin to consider what history to relate, what stories to tell, what quotations to cite, what headlines to notice, what issues to remind people of, what real-life examples to give. Those who meditate on Jesus feeding the five thousand near the Sea of Galilee are bound to think not only of that miraculous event but also of how God fed his rebellious people in the desert long years before. They will also recollect how, later, Jesus spoke similar words to his friends at the Last Supper, identifying the bread and wine with his body and blood given for them and the world. Finally, they will recognize that these actions and words are at the very heart of our own Christian fellowship today. All this is reflected in John's account of the event (John 6). Meditation on the texts of Scripture frequently calls to mind the past, illuminates the present and brings before us new possibilities for the future.

4 *Imagine*

Bishop James Tengatenga of Southern Malawi believes that preaching calls for an exercise in imagination. At the National Service of Worship in 2001, he said,

> Can we *imagine* a politics of justice and compassion in place of the present global politics of oppression and economic idolatry? Dare we *imagine* an economics of equality and care in place of the dominant economics of affluence and poverty? Can we *imagine* what would happen if we began to nurture our children with prophetic vision and with biblical dreams? (Ross 2004:103)

The text of the Bible leads both preacher and people to dream dreams and to realize that things don't have to remain as they are. The bishop was preaching about social and political justice, but the same procedure is used to arouse personal faith, to change people's behaviour and to create compassion and love.

Imagination was the key to Kivengere's preaching (see p. 52). Since the Bible is a pictorial book, with little abstract material, he used picture-language to bring people near to Jesus. He wanted every listener to meet Jesus for themselves, in God's way, not the preacher's.

> He would begin with a deceptively simple story, then fill it in with splashes of humour, a stroke of pathos, a touch of the everyday – and people suddenly see their own reflection coming into view on the canvas, and the love of Christ reaching out. (Coomes, 1990:252)

In some parts of the world, preachers' imaginations have run riot. This is quite allowable, but we do need to exercise some discernment and restraint in order to see what is a legitimate application of the text, and what is not. Question 17 in the Study Suggestions at the end of this chapter helps you to reflect on this, using the following examples:

(a) Exodus 25.20 – see p. 74.
(b) Luke 19.5: Like Zacchaeus, we need to 'come down', to be humble if we are to meet Jesus.
(c) Mark 6.48: Like the disciples, we struggle with life's storms and need Jesus to be with us.
(d) Genesis 24.58: 'Will you go with this man?' used as an appeal to people to accept Jesus.
(e) Genesis 43.27: 'The old man of whom you spoke; is he still alive?' used in connection with Colossians 3.9, 10 (KJV) in order to urge Christians to be sanctified by putting off the old nature.
(f) Joshua 2.18: The scarlet thread which saved Rahab speaks of the saving blood of Christ.
(g) Luke 10.33: The Samaritan is Christ who left two coins (baptism and the Eucharist) with the innkeeper (the clergy) at the inn (the Church) for the care of the saved man (the believer).

(Most of the above are 'allegories', in which every part of the story is a symbol of something else in real life. The last comes from one of Augustine's sermons, even though he told preachers that they should preach on the meaning of the text intended by the original author.)

Imagination helps to set us free from thinking we always have to 'tell' people what to do. Using our imagination to remind them of what God has done and is doing is much more likely to lead to change in behaviour (see p. 24).

5 *The silences*

Bishop K. H. Ting, of China, reminds us to pay attention not only to what the Bible says, but also to what it does *not* say (Sugirtharajah, 1991:454). Very often writers in the Bible leave us with a question to which we would love to know the answer. But it is we who must answer, and that is the challenge which the Bible leaves with us. Here are some examples:

- Mark 16.8 is where the Gospel of Mark ends, according to the most reliable manuscripts. Scholars have suggested a number of reasons why Mark failed to write any more, but perhaps he intended to leave it just there. The women 'said nothing to anyone, for they were afraid' – perhaps you, my readers, feel like they did, and perhaps you will be afraid to witness to all that Jesus has done for you. We know that the women eventually overcame their fear, and shared the news of the resurrection with Jesus' disciples – otherwise you and I would not have Mark's Gospel and be reading it today. Will you also share the good news?

- Luke 15.32 is where the parable of the Prodigal Son ends – but there were *two* sons. What happened to the elder brother? Did he continue to sulk because his father was so kind to his good-for-nothing brother? Or did he finally join in the welcome party? We do not know – but we can at least know how we should act and share God's gladness over bad people whose lives are changed by Jesus.

- Jonah is the one book in the Bible which ends with a question mark.

  > God asks Jonah a question, but the Bible does not tell us Jonah's reply . . . And why is this? We must realize, this is not only a question God asked of Jonah. Even more so, He is asking it of us. And He is waiting eagerly for our answer. (Sugirtharajah, 1991:455)

- Esther is a book which does not mention the name of God. But it commends Esther for her courage, loyalty and kindness, even though we read nothing about her religious practices. This silence tells us that there are some things which are more important than religion – though religion, at its best, ought to help us to be like Esther.

There are other examples of questions which are not answered in Luke 13.23, John 21.21, Matthew 24.3 and Acts 1.6. If they are to be faithful to the text, preachers must not try to answer all these questions, for this is the work of the people themselves. Once this was done very powerfully by an artist. Holman Hunt's famous picture, *The Light of the World*, shows Jesus standing outside a house, knocking at the door. But the door has no handle. Hunt said that the door can be opened only by the person inside, for this was Hunt's imaginative illustration of Revelation 3.20.

> On Calvary Jesus preached the final sermon in almost complete silence. This word could not be misunderstood. It could be ignored, rejected, but not misunderstood. It was perfect communication at infinite cost. Hence the preacher who looks to Jesus as a model had better count the cost. I suppose the point I'm trying to make is that the distinguishing feature of the Christian preacher . . . is not silver-tongued eloquence or elegant sermon structure, but the marks he or she bears in their body of the dying of the Lord Jesus. (Morris, 1996:39)

Preachers' Classes

Every preacher needs help. Preachers cannot expect to have original thoughts all the time, but they ought to be ready to borrow themes, ideas, stories and illustrations from any source. The contents of this book come from many different people in many different countries, and so should the contents of our sermons. People will find it more interesting than having to listen every Sunday to the constantly repeated ideas of one person. So preachers should keep their eyes and ears open all the time to resources that come from outside. Books are an obvious resource, but so are people. Busy preachers don't have much time to listen to other people's sermons, but they could well listen to one another in seminars, fellowships or deanery meetings. Education is a good thing to have, but even the best-educated preachers will need to refresh their minds continually.

But some pastors, especially in towns, are aware that their congregation may be better educated than they are. Educated people expect to be spoken to in excellent English, French, Spanish, Swahili, Tamil or Mandarin. They expect beautifully constructed sermons with biblical scholarship and informed comment on current affairs. Pastors who are aware of their shortcomings often try to avoid such congregations; and sometimes even the congregations look down on the preacher. This used to be a common problem in large African parishes where there would be one trained pastor and perhaps a dozen lay preachers or teachers. It is becoming a problem even in Europe as fewer trained clergy have to rely on more and more lay readers. Several solutions to this problem have been found.

First, education does not make a preacher. A Nigerian preacher with a doctorate in divinity spoke in impeccable English, quoting widely from good literature and showing he was abreast of the latest theological scholarship – and the result was a lifeless sermon which bored everyone (Sundkler, 1960:122). By contrast, Zechariah Msonga, a young man with little education, working as cathedral caretaker, went to a meal at the home of Festo and Mera Kivengere in Dodoma in 1947. As a result, his home life was transformed and he became an evangelist (Coomes, 1990:150f.). Eventually he travelled all over East Africa until the end of his long life. His preaching had the anointing of the Holy Spirit, and no one was ever bored, however much education they had!

Second, this problem is sometimes solved by special circumstances. In South Africa the system of apartheid made all black people brothers and sisters, whatever their education level. It even brought their non-black Christian brothers and sisters close to them because everyone, whatever their skin colour, felt that they were oppressed and hurt by apartheid. Any experience of oppression puts ministers and people all on the same level – because all are equally downtrodden (Sundkler, 1960:122).

A third solution to the problem is a programme of preachers' training given by the pastor. In Dabon, Cote d'Ivoire, 275 catechists used to gather every Saturday to hear the pastor's sermon, and then they would go out to preach it themselves in the villages next day (Sundkler, 1960:164). The Methodist Church used to draw up a quarterly preaching plan, with sermon outlines. A South African Bible school once used to publish 5,000 copies a month of *The Preacher's Help* in many different languages. It contained two-page outlines of sermons, with some notes on the biblical text, for use on Sundays (Sundkler and Steed, 2000:669).

Kurewa (2000:154) suggests that pastors plan regular one- or two-day retreats with their lay readers in order to equip them to preach not on their favourite texts (yet again!) but on the Church's lectionary, or on national events or festivals (e.g. the annual 'Children's Sunday' in India), or on major issues of the day. They will need the pastor's help if they are to make such sermons truly expository of texts of the Bible.

It is undoubtedly true that most of those preaching on any Sunday are not pastors but lay people. They stand in the tradition of the prophets of the Old Testament, all lay people except Ezekiel, who were often called by God to denounce corrupt priests and kings. Lay preachers have two big advantages over the professional pastor. First, they preach not for pay but for love, so everyone knows they must believe what they are saying. Second, they may not have had much theological training, but they have their ears closer to the ground where ordinary people walk; they hear their cries and share their pain, poverty and hunger or whatever may be affecting their lives at the time.

Study Suggestions

1 What languages do you know? What texts have you been helped to understand by comparing different versions of the Bible in different languages?

2 Consider the historical situations of the writers of Isaiah 55.1–3 and Matthew 2.1–12. In today's world, can you think of any people who are in situations like these?

3 See 'Culture' (p. 98). What other words or ideas in the New Testament may need explaining to the ordinary person in your culture?

4 In Luke's Gospel, compare 9.50 with 11.23, and 12.37 with 17.8 – what accounts for the apparent contradictions here?

5 See p. 102 (2). Find other passages where Paul freely expressed his feelings. How far do you think today's preachers should do the same? Give reasons for your answer.

6 Think of a controversial issue facing your local or national church. How could you dramatize different approaches to it? Outline the drama, and the parts to be played.

7 What stories are favourites with adults and children where you live? What lessons, if any, do they teach? Choose one and say how it does the four things mentioned on p. 104.

8 Often preachers scold people or tell them what they ought to do, but the Bible speaks more of what God does. Which did you do in your last four sermons?

9 Three sermons could be preached on Mark 10.46:

   (a) Believe! because the sign shows that Jesus is the Messiah.
   (b) Be kind! because Jesus had compassion for those in need.
   (c) Bring your needs to Jesus, who invites you in your blindness.

Which of these three do you think is most true to the writer's intention; and which one do you think you should preach to your congregation?

10 (a) What was the problem of the man in the crowd in Luke 12.13–21?
   (b) What did Jesus think his problem was?
   (c) What problem did the rich man in Jesus' parable think he had?
   (d) What was his real problem?
   (e) How might each of these problems relate to the people who come to your church on Sundays?

11 What was Luke trying to do in 4.1–13? Was he:

(a) Warning Christians that they will be tempted?
(b) Showing them that the word of God will enable them to overcome temptation?
(c) Guiding missionaries not to take the easy way but to follow Jesus?
(d) Helping Christians to understand and follow Jesus in Lent?
(e) Something else?

12 What is the main significance for us today of

(a) the story of the Exodus?
(b) Jesus' miraculous healings?

13 Take two parables of Jesus, one of which readily applies to your world today and one of which is difficult for people to understand. Why is this the case?

14 What is the main aim of Bailey's poem on p. 108?

15 What new insights have recently come to you in your reading of the Bible? What, or who, helped you to discover something new?

16 Outline your typical sermon preparation programme. What time do you give to prayer, listening, meditating and imagining?

17 Take the seven examples of imaginative interpretation of a Bible text (p. 114). Which do you think is legitimate interpretation and which is not? Give your reasons.

18 What do you think the following silences of Jesus meant to convey? Matthew 15.23; Mark 15.5; Luke 23.9; John 8.6; 18.9. Do you think they communicated better than words, or less well? Is there any 'silence' in the Bible which you wish the writer had answered?

19 How can educated congregations be a help to pastors, rather than a threat?

20 Outline what happens in any preaching classes which you have experienced. How could these classes be more helpful to those who attend?

7

PREACHING ON A THEME

1 Caring about Justice

Preach not because you have to say something, but because you have something to say.

Richard Whateley, Archbishop of Dublin, 1860

In recent years many church leaders in Africa, Latin America and Europe have brought hope to oppressed and hopeless people. This has often involved them in conflict with political leaders. At such times, when dictators forbid any opposition to their rule, it is the Church which has acted as the only opposition. This was the case in Nazi Germany, when the confessing Church gave teaching which was forbidden by the state, quoting Acts 5.29: 'We must obey God rather than any human authority.' One of them, Pastor Dietrich Bonhoeffer, even plotted to overthrow Hitler and was executed. The Catholic and Lutheran Churches were a God-given sign of hope to the people of Poland and East Germany under their communist oppressors. So was Archbishop Desmond Tutu during the apartheid years in South Africa. Pastor Wang Mingdao was imprisoned in China for over 20 years because of his Bible teaching. The Brazilian Dom Helder Camara was criticized by government leaders for supporting poor shanty-town dwellers. 'When I feed the poor,' he said, 'they call me a saint; when I ask why the poor are hungry, they call me a communist.' Archbishop Oscar Romero was assassinated in Nicaragua in 1981 for doing the same thing. Archbishop Janani Luwum was murdered and Bishop Festo Kivengere was exiled in 1977 for denouncing Idi Amin's crimes against the people of Uganda. They found that they could not avoid challenging politicians if Christ was to be the conscience of their country, but they never gave support to one particular political party. The life of Archbishop Pius Ncube of Bulawayo is at risk, as I write this, for exposing Mugabe's crimes in Zimbabwe.

But the Church has not always shown such courage. The Church in Rwanda failed to prevent the tribal genocide in 1994 probably because the revival had preached personal salvation, but ignored the ethical demands of the gospel and even regarded any involvement in social or political justice as 'unspiritual'. Hence preachers had never recognized the ethnic hatred and had no message for it. They were expert at denouncing individual sin but not corporate sin. In Myanmar (Burma) today, the churches keep relatively quiet about the terrible oppression of the people by the military junta – but Christians are only about 6 per cent of the total population (whereas they were a strong majority in Poland, Africa and Latin America), and so they fear they may be deprived of freedom to evangelize if they are critical of their rulers. And even in Malawi, for most of Hastings Banda's 30-year dictatorship, the churches were cowed into silence.

It is often easier to preach against injustice when the injustice is at its worst – at least then the problem is clear to everyone. This was the case before slavery was abolished in the UK and before apartheid was abolished in South Africa. Ten years before the abolition of apartheid an Englishman, feeling the Church in the UK was very sleepy, said to the Dean of Johannesburg, 'You're lucky, you've got apartheid.' In some ways, apartheid made it easier to stand up for the gospel. But even in such clear-cut cases, not all Christians join in. Some Pentecostal and independent churches would argue that politics is a dirty game in which Christians should not be involved. Their preachers claim that to discuss politics will obscure the clarity of the gospel – which they are primarily called to proclaim. They feel they are called not to try to change society directly, but to change people inwardly – then renewed Christian people will be like leaven and ultimately change society.

In 1994 the Malawian churches became the 'widely acknowledged midwives of democracy' in finally bringing Banda's rule to an end. Since then Catholics, Presbyterians, Anglicans and Pentecostals united to protect democratic values when President Muluzi attempted to stay in power beyond the constitutionally permitted two terms. Bishop Tengatenga, of Southern Malawi, said in 1998,

> We will support the government when it does good, but we will not hold our peace when it goes wrong . . . Never again will we obey the state when it tells us that the Church's role is to pray and bless the status quo . . . or when they take it upon themselves to be arbiters in the matters of God like it used to be when the state edited our sermons in the past. Never again will the Church keep quiet. (Ross, 2004:99)

Challenge is only one part of the Church's obligation; reconciliation is another, as Archbishop Tutu showed by establishing the Truth and Justice Commission after the end of apartheid in South Africa. At these public hearings, those who had committed acts of violence were asked to come forward voluntarily to confess and to receive forgiveness – on the basis of the truth. This is never easy. 'If you are going to be a bridge of reconciliation, you must be prepared to be walked on by both sides', said Bishop Festo Kivengere (Coomes, 1990:401).

This is the tradition in which Dr David Gitari, formerly Archbishop of Kenya, stood – and risked his life in doing so. His sermons on issues of national justice at times of crisis have been published in two books, *Let the Bishop Speak*, 1988, and *In Season and out of Season: Sermons to a Nation*, 1996.

Reflections
David Gitari

> Every trained preacher knows that there are many styles or methods of preaching. I am however most attracted to what is known as expository preaching . . . Expository preaching embraces both preaching and teaching. It includes sharing an understanding of the historical and spiritual context in which different Bible passages are set. Furthermore, the expository preacher would fail in his duty if he did not let the message of the Bible come alive to the modern hearer. Though written thousands of years ago, the word of God is meant to be effective in our lives today and it is the task of the preacher to make his hearers realise this fact. This process of bringing God's word to bear on our contemporary world is part of what is meant by a prophetic ministry. (Gitari, 1988:ix)

Not everyone is called to be a bishop or president of a national church as Dr Gitari was. But every preacher has the responsibility, like Dr Gitari, to show people how the Bible relates to the problems of their lives today. Jesus has a message for us now. Preachers must always make it clear that they are not using the pulpit as a platform for their own ideas, but are only opening up the word of God. If it touches on matters of justice and politics today, this is not the preacher's doing – it is the message of God. As long as preachers do not get directly involved in party politics and can show that their message comes out of the Bible, then they must follow the example of Jesus by speaking about matters of justice. Dr Gitari tells the following story to illustrate this:

> Two people were sailing in a boat. Out in the deep, one of them starts making a hole in the boat. His companion asks, 'What are you doing?' and is told to mind his own business. Well, what you are doing cannot be your own business, because when you make that hole, water will come in and you and I will sink, so I cannot allow you to make a hole in this boat. We are all part and parcel of the nation, and the Gospel persuades us to stand firm for what is true and right. (Church Mission Society, 1991)

Many political leaders in Africa are Christian believers and welcome the intervention of preachers in issues of national life. In 1987 Dr Gitari preached at the funeral of a local politician who had been murdered. Other people tried to take over the leadership of the service, but Dr Gitari pointed out that at a church burial service, the senior church minister is in charge, whether he is a bishop or a pastor. He preached strongly against the evil of murder, whatever the motive. Afterwards a Muslim political leader who had been present met Dr Gitari and introduced him to a friend with these words:

> This is Bishop Gitari, one of the most courageous bishops in this country who always speaks the truth. But as politicians it is our duty to attack him, even when we know what he is saying is true. Bishop, continue speaking the truth, even when we politicians attack you! (Gitari, 1996:64)

First, Dr Gitari based everything he said about current affairs in his sermon on careful research beforehand – he needed to be absolutely sure of his facts. Second, he rarely mentioned names of people who had wrongly oppressed the weak, but his description of the situation was such that his hearers could easily guess what and who he was referring to. Third, his sermons on sensitive or political matters always followed a written script, which could be shown to anyone who might later accuse him of saying something he did not say.

Preachers who deal with such topics should do the same – and probably also check the suitability of their message with a senior church leader beforehand. But whoever the preacher is, they will be well-advised to have a 'support-group', to guide them in their public ministry. Bishop Gitari had such a group, and it would not be easy to speak regularly to those who exercise power in the nation without such support. Such a group should consist mainly of lay people who share the preacher's love for the people. Bishop Gitari says he would have liked to give his book *Let the Bishop Speak* the title *Let the People Speak* because his aim is that ordinary Christians will see their responsibility to work for the entire well-being of everyone.

Sometimes we need to proclaim God's word about a local example of injustice, when we are not sure of all the facts. Perhaps we have heard only rumours about evil deeds. In such cases we may need to use coded language, so that our meaning is clear to those who think about it, but there is no direct and explicit application to a political event. As long as our message is manifestly biblical, as Gitari's is, people can be left to make their own application from the words being spoken and the pictures being painted. This is how Jesus replied to Pilate's question, 'Are you the king of the Jews?' Without giving an explicit answer, Jesus gave Pilate enough information to show him the nature of Jesus' kingship.

When an important politician, J. M. Kariuki, was murdered in March 1975, Bishop Gitari was due to give a series of talks on the radio. He decided to explain the sanctity of human life by expounding the Kenyan national anthem which begins, 'Oh God of all creation, bless this land and our nation, justice be our shield and defender'. As a result he was summoned to appear at the Ministry of Information who told him, 'Your sermons this week have been very disturbing. You said that the cries of the blood of Abel (Genesis 4.10) have reached heaven; people might think you are talking about Kariuki.' Gitari replied, 'Mr Chairman, if the sermons have been disturbing, then they have served their purpose. The gospel is disturbing to sinners, and what I am really saying is, if you are created in God's image, no one should kill you. Sir, you are created in God's image; nobody should kill you' – and he pointed a finger at each person in the room. Then the chairman said, 'If that is the case, continue!'

Another feature must be noted about Dr Gitari's preaching. He is primarily making biblical, not political, points about justice. In this his preaching is different from the speeches of Dr Martin Luther King Jr and Dr Allan Boesak on pp. 88–90. He is convinced from his reading of the Bible and his discipleship of Christ that God loves his creation and has made human beings stewards of it. God is angry with injustice, favours the poor and weak, and sets people free from fear and oppression not just in a future life, but here and now. That is what Jesus did. Also like Jesus, Gitari uses his imagination to let well-known stories speak about people and situations today. A story about Jethro's advice to Moses (Exodus 18) becomes a picture of a bishop managing his diocese; an emperor becomes a president of a nation; a small farmer (1 Kings 21) becomes a victim of today's land-grabbers. This use of story is especially suitable to African culture, but it is also much needed – and underused – in Western churches. When it is used, people appreciate it (see p. 52).

Politicians often tell preachers, 'Stay out of politics.' But preaching the message of Jesus involves us in pointing out ways in which powerful people are spoiling God's creation, just as Archbishop Tutu and Dr Boesak did in apartheid South Africa. It is very risky to do this – Bishop Gitari even had government agents try to kill him in his house. But to keep silent about such abuses is also to take a 'political' position – by supporting evil actions.

In 1978, when Daniel arap Moi became President of Kenya, he developed a new political philosophy for the nation. It was called the *Nyayo* philosophy. The word *nyayo* was not well known in Kenya at that time. It is Swahili for 'footsteps', and Moi's purpose was that all should follow the political example set by his predecessor, Jomo Kenyatta, and the KANU party. In fact, the word is used in the Swahili Bible in 1 Peter 2.21. This new word, heard every day in Kenya, was a gift for preachers all over the land. Peter speaks about being prepared to suffer for the sake of truth and righteousness like Jesus did. These are the *nyayo* that we should follow. It can even be linked to the Kenyan government's official policy to fight against poverty, ignorance and disease. It therefore becomes a ready-made challenge, out of the Bible, to seek the welfare of marginalized people. It is completely loyal to Kenyan government policy, but it implies strong criticism of any leaders who betray the moral standards which the country says it is following. It also links with the heart of the gospel, which says that it is Christ's suffering which brought about salvation and healing for human beings.

2 Caring about Creation

And hark how blithe the throstle sings;
He too is no mean preacher.
Come forth into the light of things;
Let Nature be your teacher.
William Wordsworth

In August 2002, a great conference was held in Johannesburg, attended by 20,000 delegates from all over the world, to discuss the theme of 'sustainable development'. This term is used to express humankind's responsibility to meet the needs of people today without endangering the ability of future generations to meet their own needs. The urgent need for the nations of the world to act together is widely recognized – simply for the survival of the human race.

Christians, however, have a special mandate to care for creation. This is reflected in the first three chapters of the Bible. This theme is echoed also in the Qur'an. See Surah 16.3–18; 23.12–22; 56.57–74, where the things God created are signs (ayat) to people. Human beings have responsibilities towards God, towards one another and towards the created order. They discharge these responsibilities whenever they are creative, artistic and scientific, and whenever they conserve the fruitfulness of the earth and develop its potential in productivity (Genesis 1.25; 2.15). Human beings come from the earth and belong to it. Because they are made in the image of God, to be like him, they must respect all equally, whatever their race or caste, religion, wealth or gender may be. God's basic gifts – air, land, water – belong not to us to buy or sell, but to God (Leviticus 25.23) and must be made available to all. There is no shortage of material here for many sermons for the subject is unquestionably relevant to the most urgent needs of all hearers. It is a theme about which Christians can agree with many people of other faiths.

The paragraphs that follow are a shortened version of a biblical exposition of these themes by Dr Vinoth Ramachandra, in two parts. First, he considers the ecological issues facing the world. Then he expounds Isaiah 11.1–10, which takes the form of a Bible study rather than a sermon, but the material could be easily adapted to take shape as a number of sermons.

Integral Mission
Vinoth Ramachandra

Concern for justice and the environment frequently go hand-in-hand. Wars have arisen in recent years over control of oil and diamonds, but the severest conflict may soon arise over access to clean water. Deforestation or overgrazing of cattle leads to soil erosion, which leads to the expansion of deserts, which leads to migration of populations, which strains the ability of richer countries to deal with the refugee crisis, which, in turn, leads to war. Arms dealers get rich by selling weapons to oppressive dictators or to greedy exploiters, or even to terrorists. People fight to secure scarce commodities, and sustainable development becomes a forgotten dream. Brazilian and Indonesian forests are destroyed to make way for cash crops or beef for export. Many animal species are threatened with extinction, and fossil fuels result in global warming, leading to catastrophic climate change – droughts and floods. The poor get poorer while the rich get richer, in the short term; but in the long run they too will suffer as much as the poor.

A white child born in New York will consume and waste more in her lifetime than 50 children born in a developing country – but it will be the poor children who die first. But to be good stewards of all the planet's resources is the responsibility of all, poor and rich alike, for we are now all dependent on one another. Christian preachers know that the gospel has the power to liberate men and women from greed and make them long for the welfare of all humanity.

Isaiah 11.1–10: An Exposition

After the destruction of Assyria, the prophet sees God's rule coming to the earth through a king on whom his Spirit rests. Out of the house of David will come a *shoot* (v. 1) – another David. He is to be the promised Messiah, whose rule will have the following features:

1 *Delight in submission to God* (vv. 2, 3)
  'The fear of the LORD' refers to our grateful reliance upon him. Wise leaders derive their wisdom from him, and this sort of wisdom results in humility and justice (Proverbs 8.12–16). Tyrannical or weak rulers arise because they do not listen to God's word.
2 *Justice for the poor* (vv. 3b–5)
  Rulers who have learned God's ways feel anger against injustice and compassion for the oppressed. The Lord champions the cause of the weak against the strong and the poor against the rich. The Lord's

anointed will rule with *righteousness* and *faithfulness* (v. 5). The Israelites saw these characteristics in their God and longed to see them in
their king also.

3 *Ecological peace* (vv. 6–9)
Human *shalom* is bound up with the *shalom* of the earth. When
the Messiah brings justice, he will also bring to an end all violence
against the earth and the animal creation. Creation will be renewed,
danger and violence will be banished, helpless and innocent people
can play with those who were once excessively greedy. The curse of
Eden is removed and the enmity between the woman's seed and the
serpent is gone (v. 8). This is the day for which the creation waits 'in
eager expectation' (Romans 8.18). Paul looks forward to the fulfilment of Isaiah's prophecy in a cosmic salvation (Romans 8.20, 21).

4 *The earth filled with the knowledge of God* (vv. 9b, 10)
The transformed Eden is also Mount Zion, which fills the whole world.
Men and women enjoy peace, holiness and the knowledge of God
through Jesus the Messiah, not through their religions. He will be the
focus of the people's search for God. Note that he is not only the *shoot*
(descendant) of David; he is also his *root*, i.e. his first ancestor. Here
is a message which makes sense in the cultures of Africa and China.

Notice that stage 4 of Dr Ramachandra's prophecy ties in with the first stage.
God's plan for his creation begins with:

• Listening humbly to God's word; *and goes on to*
• The promotion of justice, at home and globally, *and*
• Care for the earth; *and finishes with*
• Enjoying and sharing the gospel of Jesus the Messiah among all
  the nations.

These are themes for preachers of every age and in every place.

The Care of Creation
David Gitari

In 1991 a county council in Kenya allocated a large part of an area of natural
beauty to two local politicians who had posed as development companies. On
this occasion Bishop David Gitari preached in the local church on 1 Kings
21.1–29. This sermon had a twin theme – the issue of justice and the issue of
care for the environment. Here are some extracts from it (1996:102–10).

King Ahab wanted to extend his vegetable garden by buying a piece
of land which a peasant farmer called Naboth had inherited from his
fore-fathers. But Naboth said No! It would have been wrong for Naboth
to sell his ancestral inheritance, even to the king. Sometimes we have to

choose – to obey people, or to obey God (see Acts 4.19, 20). Land is a precious commodity and it is the duty of the County Council to exercise good stewardship of the land entrusted to it for the benefit of all people.

In February, two applications came before the Council to develop Kamuruana Hill for profit. These applications were approved. There was not a single Naboth to say No! But there are two reasons why this land should not be given to developers who want to extend their vegetable gardens. First, a beautiful forest covered the hill, but this was cut down five years ago and since then the clouds have moved away. No replanting has been done. The hill was created so that all of us can enjoy its beauty, but it is now 'groaning with pain' at its nakedness (see Rom. 8.19) – in spite of the fact that one of the Ruling Party's stated objectives is the preservation of the environment. Second, land entrusted to the County Council should not be given to greedy land-grabbers when it could alleviate the poverty of the hundreds of people who have no land at all. Our Church is even prepared to send its young people now to help to replant trees on the hill for the benefit of the community.

There are at least eight examples of public land being given away to rich land-owners. Allow me to enumerate them [Dr Gitari briefly describes each case, with this refrain after each one:] . . . and there was no Naboth to say No! If the Councillors are no longer capable of saying No! to land-grabbers, then they have outlived their usefulness and may as well call it a day!

When Naboth said No! the king went away depressed. But Queen Jezebel plotted to get Naboth falsely accused of things he had not done, without the opportunity to defend himself. Then she wrote letters in the king's name ordering Naboth to be killed. The elders did not bother to find out that the letters were forged, but simply followed them as orders from 'above'. Often in Kenya injustice has been done on the basis of orders from 'above'. Ahab took possession of the murdered Naboth's land – but God commanded the prophet Elijah to go and confront him. In an earlier story Ahab had called Elijah 'You troubler of Israel' because Elijah denounced the sin of the king. But it is not the prophets or the preachers who are the troublers of the people; it is the land-grabbers, the Councillors, the exploiters of the poor, the destroyers of our beautiful environment.

The end of the story, however, is that the king repented in sack-cloth. And our God is a forgiving God. He forgives us if we turn away from the evil. And don't think I am just talking about those who gave away our hillside; we have all sinned in one way or another. For example, many of us have allowed bad things to be done in our society without raising our voices in protest. But God will forgive us, every one, if we only turn back to Jesus, who died that we might be forgiven.

It is important to note several points about this sermon.

1 *Dr Gitari constantly referred back to the text of Scripture – the word was not his but God's.*

2 *He had also done extensive research on the local situation – all he said was accurate.*

3 *People understood very well the situations he was talking about – the sermon related to their lives.*

4 *He stressed the responsibility of us all to care for creation and he supported this from the Bible.*

5 *He finished by offering restoration and hope – not simply condemnation.*

6 *God's message of mercy was not just for the bad people – but for absolutely everyone.*

When sermons on justice or on the environment are characterized by these features, then it is possible for anyone to preach in this way, not just distinguished church leaders.

Study Suggestions

1 Paul told his Roman readers to 'be subject to the governing authorities' (Rom. 13.1). What would you want to say to Christians in today's world about their responsibilities to the state? How could you do so by expounding Romans 13.1–7?

2 What sort of political issues should the Church get involved in? What are the arguments for and against this? If the Church is involved, should this be the role of Christians in general, or pastors, or just the chief leaders?

3 What principles did Bishop Gitari follow in his preaching?

4 Do you feel there are any issues of injustice or exploitation which the Church needs to preach against:

(a) in your country;
(b) in your district?

If the Church does this, how far will it get the support of the people?

5 See 1 Peter 2.21. What actual footsteps did Peter want his readers to follow? What Bible passages, if any, make links with government policies or current issues in your country?

6 What major environmental issues:

(a) have you heard a lot about recently; and
(b) are confronting people where you live?

How can preachers help listeners to see the issues and take action?

7 What do the first three chapters of Genesis teach us about human stewardship of God's creation?

8 A Nigerian Christian leader said, 'It is the rich nations of America and Europe who are polluting the earth. It is they who should change their ways – it's not our responsibility in the developing world.' Do you agree with him? If not, why not?

9 Isaiah 11 is a text much used at Christmas time. How effectively do you think Dr Ramachandra has used it as an incentive to environmental responsibility?

10 Many people in all countries of the world suffer unjustly as Naboth did. What examples of human greed, for wealth or power, do you see around you today, and how can you in your ministry make a difference?

8

PREACHING IN THE SLUMS OF BRAZIL
Siméa de Souza Meldrum

Don't ask what the Church can do for the poor; ask what the poor can do for the Church.
We still suffer from the effects of what the Church has done to communities rather than with them.

Faith in the City, London, 1985

Every culture is organized on the basis of its collective sacred system of beliefs by which the people live and understand the realities of life. Everything in the culture – the value of the human being, the family, relationships, laws, ethical questions, the value of science and work, economic questions, morality and justice, the place of God in society, etc. – will be built on these foundations. Communities are ruined when they are built on a foundation of ignorance and lies; they develop when they are built on knowledge and truth.

The more a culture is built on the biblical vision of truth, the more it will manifest justice, peace, prosperity, solidarity, equity, development and life. In other words, the nearer it will be to the kingdom of God. We know that no culture will realize the kingdom of God completely before the return of Christ, but our aim is to fight for its realization in our lives and communities: 'Your kingdom come' (Luke 11.20).

As the Church of God, it is our task 'to go and make disciples'. In preaching truth and bringing knowledge, we will confront and destroy the work of the Evil One in our culture. The nature of the Evil One is to lie, both to individuals and to nations (Revelation 20.3). When we look at different cultures, we find many lies generally accepted, which produce certain values in individuals and communities.

There are positive and negative elements in Brazilian culture. The Church needs to identify and to affirm the positives, and to replace the negatives with truth and knowledge. Some of the first Christian missionaries made the mistake of not affirming the positives, e.g. the natural instincts of hospitality and joy. As a result, the gospel appeared to many Brazilians to mutilate their culture, and to oppress rather than to liberate them.

False Assumptions of Brazilian Culture

Siméa believes that the preacher's first task is to understand the culture and problems of the people. Therefore she begins by identifying several false popular assumptions.

We who work in very poor communities like the garbage tip of Olinda, Pernambuco, can state some of the untruths that affect our community and that we are having to fight against. For example:

- Brazil cannot hope to change, for 'He who is born a lizard can never become an alligator.'
- This is our destiny, for 'Wood that grows crooked will die crooked.'
- Your worth is measured by what you have.
- Let us eat, drink and be merry for tomorrow we die.

These concepts are found in other parts of the world, but they are accepted in Brazil because the political administration leads people to believe in them. These popular assumptions bind these communities into degenerative situations, ruining their lives and their hopes of future change.

Other examples are as follows:

- Indian (= aboriginal, or native), black and rural people are inferior. Although racism is a criminal offence in Brazil, the concept of racial inferiority is clearly present in society. A slavish mentality gives support to this system. It is linked to animism, in which there are superior and inferior beings because the gods have made them thus. Also spiritism, a strong religion in Brazil, believes in a karma that people are born with, in which inferiors must in some way serve their superiors. Although this is not verbalized, it is clearly seen in day-to-day life.
- Men are worth more than women. This belief emphasizes the inferiority of the woman and manifests itself in society through a macho culture, for example: 'A woman is more sinful than a man', 'A woman is less intelligent than a man', 'The woman alone serves to heat her belly at the stove and to cool it in the tank washing clothes', 'The woman is an object of the bed and the kitchen', etc.
    This belief has been one of the biggest causes in Brazil of reducing the woman to a sex object and the consequences have been tragic:

pregnancy outside marriage, abandonment of children, prostitution for survival, adolescent pregnancy, growth of the slums, street population, etc.

- Work is a curse. Here in Brazil, many times work is seen as a curse to be endured and not a blessing to help people to be creative and self-supportive for the glory of God. 'Inferiors are created to work for their superiors.' The aim of the Brazilian man is to become the boss, or to have his own business, in order to work less. When somebody obtains a job, it soon becomes clear that he develops the desire to show his power. His status is raised. He starts getting into debt, thus affirming that he is now of the consumer class – but soon he will become so indebted that he will have to return to the inferior classes.

- The government is responsible. This is yet another example of a slavish mentality. People say, 'The few give the orders and have all the responsibility for conducting things' – and so ordinary people take no responsibility. 'The task is the Government's and not mine, I do not have co-responsibility, I cannot change anything, and I depend on the others for my life and my future.'

- All roads lead to God. This popular lie is found in Brazilian religious syncretism. Each road states its own truth. Many people assume they are Christians just because they have been baptized, yet they still practise spiritism and believe in reincarnation. The Church has to confront this false belief with the truth of the Word of God.

Preaching to Those Excluded from the Development of Society

Having identified the problem, Siméa goes on to show how the word of God is an antidote to despair.

The key word of the gospel of Jesus Christ to these communities is 'hope'. 'Now faith, hope, and love abide, these three; and the greatest of these is love' (1 Corinthians 13.13). Hope is our expectation of the good things God will do. It is very common to give greater emphasis to faith and love, and to undervalue hope. But, in our case to raise up hope is to show how transformation can begin in the individual and in the community. Therefore a hopeful person not only hopes, but also is full of glad expectation. We are called by the God of hope: 'May the God of hope fill you with all joy and peace in believing, so that you may abound in hope by the power of the Holy Spirit' (Romans 15:13). It is this God whom we must proclaim within the communities of extreme need. We need to ask ourselves if we are really bringing this hope. Otherwise our faith will dry up and our love will be without direction and fruit.

So how can we preach hope? 'We also boast in our sufferings, knowing that suffering produces endurance, and endurance produces character, and character produces hope' (Romans 5.3–4). This is the only way to the hope that the Bible offers. The development of hope will always depend on the way we face tribulation. Nobody needs to look for tribulation because life here in Brazil is full of tribulations. The secret lies in how we deal with them. Each time I manage to overcome a tribulation, holding on firmly to the hand of God, I add a little to the hope in my life. Each time I take hold of more perseverance, the more my character and integrity grows. What we say becomes more consistent with what we believe and do. The peace that comes from within is being expressed and is becoming stronger than the surrounding circumstances.

After ten years of trying to understand the garbage tip community and to learn how to teach a transforming gospel, we have found many failings in the Church's preaching to our communities. For example, the ever-changing membership of the churches suggests that the preaching is not addressing all the needs of the people, and has even raised false expectations. Some people who are in the Church start to grow but they arrive at a point where they question if God is really involved with their needs, because they continue unemployed, without quality of life or hope of improvement. For these people the next plate of food is their immediate problem and they are still afraid to face the cultural defects mentioned above. So they lose momentum and start to search for solutions in their own strength. Many of them are tempted to give up. We do not want to fall into the error of patronizing the poor with easy words, without any realistic strategy. We see that the proclamation of the gospel has to be integrated with a programme of citizenship training and generation of work and income.

In Luke 12.35–48, we find many beautiful images of hope. There the servants are expectantly waiting for the return of their Lord, prepared for service. Those who long in their hearts for their Lord's return wait in a different way from those who do not. Only those who long for his return and who manage to wait with good heart, even if he is late, will meet him. Those who do not watch and wait have built their hopes on 'false personal expectations that are far too high'. They do not see 'the work of God in their lives', but prefer to use God to obtain their pet projects; in other words they are still relating to God as if they were dealing with animistic gods – with bargaining and manipulation.

In Matthew 25.1–13, we find the ten virgins waiting for the groom. Five of them are prepared for the wait, even if the groom is delayed.

The other five leave their places and are distracted by their personal expectations, and they miss the party. It is interesting to note that the five cautious ones do not want to share their oil with the five fools. This teaches us that some things cannot be shared. Everyone has to develop their own character in which there must be a space for hope to develop.

When I arrived on the garbage tip ten years ago, everything seemed difficult, even impossible. But as time went on I began to understand that the fault was in me. I did not know how to have hope to create hope in these hopeless people, and so God started to work in me first. He showed me that I must learn to depend on him alone, and not rely on earthly resources; and if I had not accepted this challenge there would be no Anglican work on the garbage tip. During all these years I have asked the bishop for financial help which he has not been able to give me. All that we have done until now has been with gifts that came from personal friends at home and abroad because the actual community has no resources to raise the funds to support the work of the ministries we are developing. During this time I learned to wait in hope, add perseverance to my character and trust only in God. As a result, God directs everything and I only have to wait with expectation and joy in my heart.

I also learned that it takes time to reach this point. I have been able to show this way of hope to other people whom God has also called to serve in this place. They also struggle to add this waiting, this perseverance and this hope to their hearts. I also suffer because I cannot share my oil with them because it is a personal gift from God to serve in this way.

From time to time we need to be reminded of the source of our hope, so that tiredness, suffering and delay do not become discouragement and despair. We need to look to the word of God where we find strength and help to continue. We may become despondent but Jesus never does: 'He will not grow faint or be crushed until he has established justice in the earth' (Isaiah 42.4). The truth is that Jesus is seeing all that we are going through and he is not discouraged. On the contrary, he is working for us and with us, which is something worth meditating on.

At times the actual battles lead us to despair but we must remember God permits these battles for a reason. We may think that the enemy is creating conflict or that other people are against our work, but the truth is that God has created us to share with him in the big plans he has for his creation. We need the fights and challenges so that the character of Christ may be formed within us. This fighting spirit must be part of the growing Christian community.

The Effect of Preaching in People's Lives

Siméa shows how preaching involves a strategic vision. Preachers find first that their own thinking and attitudes are changed. They realize that they need to receive help from other fellow-workers. They begin to identify with the poor and accept the reality of the ministry of the poor to them.

When the gospel of our Lord Jesus Christ is preached, not only the individual lives of men, women and children are transformed, but also the whole local community begins to change, as people with new attitudes begin to infiltrate the community with new standards.

The slum is a place where the poor and the excluded from society live. Generally more than 70 per cent do not have a fixed income, and manage to survive through the help of neighbours or donations from the public as they pass by on the streets. The slums [or *favelas* as they are known in Brazil] appear overnight, without any planning or proper amenities such as water, electricity and sewage. Little by little the government begins to implant the infrastructure that any community needs. Schools, crèches and community support services appear, but only as and when the local community goes out in search of what is rightfully theirs. Many of these dwellers originate from the countryside where running water and electricity are not the norm, and so little is done to insist on such installations in the newly formed *favela*. These people bring no professional skills so have little to offer to the work market. Others have passed through prison and are excluded from the development system.

I have been serving in the Olinda Rubbish Tip since 1993. In the beginning it was difficult to persuade others to join me. Violence and total misery was the norm, and even the local government were un-interested in helping, as it was not a vote-catching place to spend their limited resources. The local town mayor commented as I began, 'Siméa, you should look for a different community to work in, we cannot contribute anything here. The problem is very complex and the town hall does not have the resources or any plans to start here.'

But Jesus declared, 'Blessed are you who are poor for yours is the kingdom of God' (Luke 6.20). The poor have a key role to play in the preaching of the gospel and in the kingdom of God, as the kingdom belongs to the poor and all social classes need to join them. 'Remember the poor' (Galatians 2.10).

Jesus' preaching to the poor was evidence that he was the Messiah (Luke 7.22). When he spoke of 'the year of the Lord's favour' (Luke 4.19), he was referring to the Year of Jubilee, which included the free-ing of slaves, the cancellation of debt and the returning of land to the poor. With Jesus, the kingdom of God became the fulfilment of this ancient law, not just in words, but in liberating actions towards the poor in all areas of life. The churches' tendency to limit liberation to mere words and salvation of the soul is not true to his message. We must not fall into the trap of preaching a gospel that has no power to transform the slum environment and a poor community.

We desperately need to help the poor throughout our lives. Contrary to common thought, the poor serve as an example to us, not the other way round. God chose the poor to serve as an example to the rich, as when Jesus saw a poor widow putting all she had into the offering (Mark 12.41–4). From this we learn the values of the kingdom of God: generosity, dependence on God, interdependence with our neighbours, submission and humility. In preaching we take something of value to the poor and in return receive from them treasures of the kingdom that can only be found hidden in the slums among those who are excluded by society as a whole. They show us our own weaknesses and fears, leading us to depend, like them, on God alone (see John 9.13–34).

The Difference that Preaching Made on the Rubbish Tip

Finally, Siméa has seen big changes. Those who were once objects of mission have now become missionaries themselves.

The poor of Olinda are no longer the excluded, ignored, dirty and violent people that they used to be. Now they are environmental preservation agents, expert recyclers, respected and key players, who are bringing new answers to hunger and misery. They are creating and developing new programmes, bringing work and generating wealth through the recycling of household and commercial waste that previously was destined to become an open tip, with all the consequent environmental damage that such places cause. These men and women are now alert to the big multinational companies that want to invade our country and remove the source of income from thousands of mothers and fathers who use the recycling materials as their principal form of income. Our sorters today travel to debate with the federal government and with other sorters from other states when, before the gospel was preached among them, they were only the dirty people rejected by society.

The young people, too, have been transformed. Before, they were restless and without prospects. Today, many of them are active in their studies, as well as key members of the Church. They feel called to witness in newly acquired secular professions or even move into full-time ministry in outreach to other nations. Transformed by the gospel of Jesus Christ today they are considered model citizens in the local community. Performing in a worship band or theatre and dance groups brings them new prestige within the wider community. They are living signs of the kingdom of God. Some who previously danced in houses of prostitution, or became hopelessly drunk and lived in warring gangs, are today young people with a purpose, and when they speak the whole community takes notice. Perhaps the most exciting change taking place is that now the Christian community that has formed from the people of the rubbish tip is moving out with the gospel challenge to the middle and upper classes. Today, Living Waters Church is planting cell groups throughout the city of Olinda, as the challenge of a people totally transformed is causing others to sit up and pay attention to the transforming message of the gospel of the kingdom, present and active within each one who chooses to receive Jesus Christ as Lord and Saviour.

Study Suggestions

1 What positive elements in your culture should the Church affirm? What negative elements, if any, should it criticize?

2 Which, if any, of the Brazilian 'falsehoods' are believed by people where you live? What other false assumptions do people hold?

3 What, according to Siméa, should be the chief elements of the Church's message to the poor?

4 What things enabled Siméa to learn to be a preacher in the slums of Olinda? What experiences have helped you to learn to preach?

5 What discouragements and conflicts might be experienced by those who preach the gospel in the slums?

6 What lessons did Siméa learn from the two parables, Luke 12.35–48 and Matthew 25.1–13? Do these parables teach you the same things, or do they teach you something else?

7 How might the following passages encourage those who are called to be slum preachers? Matthew 5.3; 12.18; 25.40; Mark 12.41–4; Luke 7.22–23; Galatians 2.10; James 2.5.

8 'In preaching we take something of value to the poor' (p. 137). What do the poor bring to us? Write an outline of a sermon on 1 Kings 17.8–16 which shows how ministers of God and poor people need one another.

9 What changes have you seen come about in the life of people through the preaching of the gospel? What changes have poor people suc-ceeded in bringing about in their locality?

FOUR SERMONS FOR REFLECTION AND EVALUATION

Note that the following four sermons are not printed here as models of excellence. They all have both strong and weak points. Readers are invited not to imitate them but to evaluate them, using the suggestions at the end of the chapter.

1 A Christmas Sermon by Karl Barth, Basel, Switzerland, 1934

Luke 2.11: Unto you is born this day a Saviour

My dear brothers and sisters, now we have heard the Christmas story. We heard about Caesar Augustus and the governor of Syria, about Joseph and Mary and the birth of the baby in Bethlehem, about the shepherds in the fields and the appearance of the angel of the Lord in their midst, about the multitude of the heavenly host, praising God and saying, 'Glory to God in the highest, and on earth peace among men with whom he is pleased!'

I surely would like to know what went on in your minds when you heard this story! Perhaps two or three among you did not listen very carefully – this happens quite often – and the story passed over their heads like a cloud or a puff of smoke. Should I read the story again for the benefit of these people of wandering thoughts? It is worth repeating twice, even a hundred times! But for today we shall leave it at this.

Or perhaps there are those, men and women, who thought I was telling a nice fairy tale, far removed from the realities of life? Too beautiful to be true? What shall I tell them? Shall I debate with them? I shall gladly do so at any other time. But presently ours is a more important task.

Perhaps also some among you, when they heard the story, were reminded of the days of their youth long since gone by. They thought of Sunday school where they were told this story for the first time, of the Christmas tree, of the presents and the candies, of how beautiful things were, but are no longer and never will be again. What shall I answer? Shall I put on a serious face and say: 'Forget about Christmas trees and Christmas sentiments and concentrate on the Christmas story itself'? This will not be my reply either.

I only intended to show you, my dear friends, that *these* are our human reactions to the Christmas story, which truly is the story of us all. It is much more important, more true and more real than all the stories in history books and novels and all the broadcast and printed news put together! A little absent-mindedness, a little unbelief and a little Christmas sentiment – these are our reactions, not only yours, but mine as well!

Until the *angel of the Lord* appears and shakes us up! The angel of the Lord most certainly passed this night through the streets and the homes and the squares of Basel. He was here for those who celebrated Christmas Eve in loneliness and distress, or on the contrary in fun and frivolity. He is here for all those who are still asleep and maybe have something to sleep off. He is passing through the churches of our town this morning. How does he tell the good news to all these people? How do they listen to him or do not listen at all? However, let us not refer to other people, but rather focus on ourselves. The angel of the Lord most certainly is here in our midst to speak and to be heard. It only remains for me to make you aware of his presence and attentive to his words, so that together we may listen, and ponder what he has to say.

An angel! That is – a *messenger*, who has some news for us. You might quite simply think of the postman bringing you some news. The angel of the Lord is God's messenger carrying the news of the Christmas story. You see, if *he* announces the news, absent-mindedness, unbelief and lofty sentiments are swept away, for the angel of the Lord descends directly from God to us. I recently saw a picture where he precipitates straight from heaven to earth, almost like lightning. Granted, this is an image, and yet it is real. If the angel of the Lord is the carrier of the news, the lightning strikes and illumines the truth: the glory of the Lord shone around them and the night was as light as the day. As the Christmas hymn has it:

> Eternal light from heaven descends,
> The earth all new and bright extends,
> And vanquished is the darkest night,
> We all may be children of light.

And now let us try to hear and understand part of what the angel of the Lord told the shepherds and tells us now. 'For to you is born this day in the city of David a Saviour!' These words – *you, this day, a Saviour* – contain the whole Christmas story. We shall meditate on each one of them.

'*To you* is born this day a Saviour', says the angel of the Lord. This is already tremendously important. First, the news of the birth of the child in Bethlehem is quite different from the news, let's say, of the arrival of the Emperor of Ethiopia in our country. You may have heard about this event. We were flattered that the emperor liked our country and that his hosts were equally impressed with their guest. But we hear this news – don't we? – thinking: 'Why should I be concerned? This is entirely a matter between him and them.' In contrast, the angel of the Lord points to Bethlehem, saying, 'for *to you* is born this day a Saviour'. For your sake God was not content to be God but willed to become human; for you he emptied himself that he may be exalted; for you he gave himself that you may be lifted up and drawn unto him. The wondrous deed brought him no gain, fulfilled no need of his. It was accomplished only for you, for us. The Christmas story then is a story that is enacted with us and for us.

The news of the birth of the child in Bethlehem is not to be likened to a statement made in a textbook. The angel of the Lord was no professor, as I am. A professor would perhaps have said, 'To mankind is born a Saviour.' So what? We are apt to deduce that mankind in general does not include me, is only meant for others. It is like in a film or a play where we are confronted with people who are not ourselves. In contrast, the angel of the Lord points to the shepherds and points to *us*. His news is directly addressed to us: '*To you* is born this day a Saviour!' You, regardless of who you are, whether or not you understand the message, whether or not you are good and pious people. The news is meant for you. For your benefit the Christmas story happened. Again, it does not take place without us; we are involved in it.

The news of the birth of the child in Bethlehem affects us differently from the morning mail. When the postman arrives, we eagerly ask: 'Anything for me?' And seizing the letter, we withdraw to read it. We resent intruders peeping over our shoulder and want to read the letter alone, since this is a private matter. In contrast, the event of Bethlehem is no private matter. '*To you* is born this day a Saviour.' True, the angel of the Lord points to you and to me individually, yet he addresses us corporately. His news ties us together like brothers and sisters who share a wonderful present from their father. No one is first, no one is last, no one gets preference, no one gets short-changed and, most important, not a single one goes wanting. He who was born in Bethlehem is the eldest brother of us all.

Therefore we pray in his name, '*Our* Father'. Therefore we do not pray, 'Give me this day my daily bread', but rather, 'Give us this day *our* daily bread'. And, 'Forgive *us our* trespasses!' And 'Lead *us* not into temptation, but deliver *us* from evil!' Therefore also we go to the

Lord's Supper as to the table of the Lord, and eat from *one* bread and drink from *one* cup. 'Take and eat! Drink ye all!' Therefore the Christian life is one great communion, a fellowship with the Saviour and hence a fellowship among brothers. Where there is no communion with the Saviour, there is no communion among brothers, and where there is no communion among brothers, there is no communion with the Saviour. The one is not possible without the other. This is the content of the angel's call '*to you*', and we should keep it in mind.

'To you – *this day*!' says the angel of the Lord. When Christ was born it was *this day*! A new day dawned in the middle of the night. Christ himself was and is the sun of this day and of every day. The new day is not only Christmas Day, it is the day of our life.

'This day' refers not only to the *past*, to 'once upon a time'. Far from it. The angel of the Lord today announces the same news he then announced to the shepherds. We live in the new day which God has made. We hear of a possible new beginning in our human relations and conditions, in the history of our lives and even in the history of the world. We are told that yesterday's misery, guilt and fear, though still existing, have been mercifully covered and no longer harm us, because to us is born a Saviour. We may take courage, pull ourselves together and venture a new start. Human experience does not warrant such confidence, yet this is the assurance of the angel of the Lord. Because the Saviour is born, therefore a new day has dawned!

'This day' implies *not only tomorrow*. Certainly *also tomorrow*! He who was born on that first Christmas Day will not die ever again but lives and reigns eternally. Yet we ought not to dwell on the morrow. You know well enough the kind of people that love to repeat: *Morgen, morgen, nur nicht heute!* (German proverb, in translation: 'Tomorrow, tomorrow, but never today!') 'Let's wait and see' is a dangerous saying. Who knows if we shall be around tomorrow? Surely the Saviour will be there, but what about us? Who knows whether we shall hear the good news once again tomorrow and shall be free to respond? The decision is not in our hands. Only yesterday I came across a word of our Swiss writer Jeremias Gotthelf: 'Life is not a light; a light can be kindled again: life is a fire given by God to burn on earth just once and never more.' My dear friends, let us pay heed lest we miss the hour of this fire right here and now. We are told elsewhere: 'O that today you would hearken to his voice! Harden not your hearts!'

This is what the angel of the Lord has to tell us when he announces '*this day*'! And now we hear: 'To you this day is born *a Saviour*'. Of the many thoughts that come to mind here, I shall choose just one.

What does the word 'Saviour' convey? The Saviour is he who brings us *salvation*, granting us all things needed and salutary. He is the helper, the liberator, the redeemer as no man, but God alone, can be and really is; he stands by us, he rescues us, he delivers us from the deadly plague. Now we live because he, the *Saviour*, is with us.

The Saviour is also he who has wrought salvation *free of charge*, without our deserving and without our assistance, and without our paying the bill. All we are asked to do is to stretch out our hands, to receive the gift, and to be thankful.

The Saviour is he who brings salvation to *all*, without reservation or exception, simply because we all need him and because he is the Son of God who is the Father of us all. 'To you this day is born a Saviour', says the angel of the Lord.

This, then, is the Christmas story. You see, we cannot possibly hear this story and not look away from ourselves, from our own life with its cares and burdens. There he is, our great God and Saviour, and here we are, human beings. And now it is true that he is for me, is for us. It is impossible to hear his story without hearing our own. It is the great *transformation* that has been worked in us once and for all, the great *joy* it has released in us, and the great *calling* we have received to set out on the way he shows us.

What shall we do now? Shall we continue in our old ways, in absent-mindedness, in disbelief, perhaps in some lofty Christian sentiments? Or shall we awake and rise, set out on our journey and turn about? The angel of the Lord does not compel anybody. Even less can I compel! A forced listening to the Christian story, a forced participation in the story, is of no avail. We must willingly listen, and willingly participate.

'And suddenly there was with the angel a multitude of the heavenly host praising God and saying, "Glory to God in the highest heaven, and on earth peace among those whom he favours."' Our place is not among the angels; we live here on earth, in this city, in this house. Yet when we hear about this song of praise and when we realize that God did not send one angel alone, but that the multitude of the heavenly host was present with their song of praise, might we not be carried away, just as we fall in step when a good band plays or unconsciously hum or whistle a well-known tune that falls on our ears? That would be it! Then we would freely listen to and freely participate in the Christmas story. Amen.

2 Remembrance Sunday, by the Revd A. A. J. Claridge, Keynsham, UK, 1986

Each year in Britain this Sunday honours the memory of those who died and suffered in war, especially the two World Wars of the twentieth century. There are military parades but the main event is the church services. These are attended by many people who never normally attend church. Therefore the service, and the sermon need to have a special character suitable for the occasion. Other countries have similar annual occasions to remember their war dead.

> In the fall of the year we are brought to remembrance.
> The unseasonal colour of the poppies stirs memories.

Back in the summer, a small boy stood with his father in a war cemetery. Rank upon rank the crosses stretched before him, the awful geometry piercing the horizon. After a moment or two's silence, he turned to his father and said, 'And you mean to tell me we won?' Faced with that panoramic vision of death, the boy could not make sense of the concept of winning and losing, victory and defeat. Hard for him to understand that nothing else was left to be done in the face of ultimate evil but to stand up and fight.

He saw only the waste. What touched him was the journey's end of so many who set out with the bloom of youth on their cheeks.

Every year I become aware that some people are increasingly uneasy about festivals of remembrance. They are not without compassion. They care about the dead and they are concerned for the living who need help. They want to support the British Legion in its work with eight million ex-servicemen and their ten million dependents. But they are uneasy about Remembrance Day services. Their unease stems from the feeling that the ceremonial may keep the idea of war alive. They worry that in this place, on this day, we may bear witness to war as something great and noble.

Their unease is sincere. They are moved, like the small boy in France, by thoughts of the frightful waste of it all. Their unease is no bad thing and should not be dismissed lightly. For the sake of the dead, for the sake of future generations, we must be clear about what we are doing this morning. Young or old, none of us can escape from the past. Whether we lived through the World Wars or not, they have shaped our present and will mould our future. The shadow of war which fell across yesterday, darkens today.

I believe we are here this morning precisely because we know war is far from glorious. From many of us it has taken so much. We realize that it is not about drums, flags and brass bands playing; it is about people dying in mud and filth and dust. It is about pain and blindness; paralysis and fear; terror and bereavement. War is the ultimate act of failure and the denial of our unique human capacity to love and be creative.

On this Remembrance Day I call to mind men and women who were caught up in conflicts for which they had no liking and certainly no military ambitions. There have been thousands upon thousands of them. They went to war because they had to go to war. Because they were so unwarlike, the most poignant memory of them is the songs they whistled and sang to keep their spirits up. They followed a long, long road a-winding not to a land of their dream, but to a nightmare.

Theirs is a courage out of my reach, and I salute them – all of them, whom the bugles called out of the sad streets and shires and who never came home. I think, too, of those who did come back, some unrecognizable, faces erased, bodies broken and minds shattered. Through their clinging to life they haunt us with the evidence of our failure. For them the cries of the poppy-sellers hang in the grey November air; pray God we have responded in full measure to their suffering and our debt to them.

Death, destruction, fear. Where is the victory? Where is the glory? For men and women lately loved, the heart cries out for an answer. They deserve more than a few fleeting moments of silence and a scattering of crimson petals on grey stones.

If this brief ceremony is all we give, then we fail them, and unease about Remembrance Day services is rightly felt. This act of remembrance takes place in a Christian church and so it speaks of peace and not of war. The Christian message is one of peace, forgiveness and reconciliation. Our Christian duty was set before us in the reading from Ephesians 4: we must throw off falsehood, speak truth to each other, we must not let anger fester nor evil thrive. We must have done with bad feelings of every kind. Above all, we must be generous to one another, forgiving one another as God in Christ forgave us.

The symbol of God's forgiveness stands in all the cemeteries where the war dead lie. That symbol is the cross and it speaks of God's love for us all, regardless of race and irrespective of human ideas of defeat or victory. The suffering of Jesus on the cross was the product of hate, expressed through the cruel ritual of death. But the love of God was also there cleansing and forgiving. His was the power which transformed the waste of death into the victory of new and continuing life.

The cross says that nothing is pointless or beyond redemption. With new strength, clearer vision and fresh determination we can and must turn hatred into love and war into peace.

The real drive for peace begins with God in the hearts and minds of people like you and me all over the world. If this morning's reveille has failed to awaken in you a firm resolve to pray for peace, to think of peace, to shout for peace and to work for peace, then all this marching and carrying of flags is an empty charade and an insult to the dead, the wounded, the widows and the orphans.

Peace begins with you and me. Make no mistake about that. Our challenge is the bringing of a divided world into love and unity; victor and vanquished alike. Time and again God has inspired men and women like us to do his work of forgiveness and reconciliation and often in the most dreadful circumstances.

Carry away with you today these words, written by an unknown prisoner in Ravensbruck concentration camp and pinned to the body of a dead child:

> O Lord, remember not only the men and women of good will, but also those of evil will. But do not remember all the suffering they have inflicted on us; remember the fruit we have borne, thanks to this suffering; our comradeship, our loyalty, our humility, our courage, our generosity, the greatness of heart which has grown out of all this, and when they come to judgement let all the fruits which we have borne be their forgiveness.

From the bottom of our hearts, in the presence of God, may we all say, 'Amen'.

3 'The Rich Fool' by Dr Martin Luther King Jr, preached in a local Baptist church (1969:67)

Dr Martin Luther King, renowned for his oratory in connection with the Civil Rights movement in the USA, was a regular Sunday preacher in ordinary local church services. Two of his sermons are reproduced here. The second has many echoes of his own 'dream' speech (see p. 88) and is prophetic of his own unfulfilled dream.

Luke 12.20, KJV: Thou fool, this night thy soul shall be required of thee

I would like to share with you a dramatic little story that is significantly relevant in its implications and profoundly meaningful in its conclusions. It is the story of a man who by all modern standards would be considered eminently successful. Yet Jesus called him a fool.

The central character in the drama is a 'certain rich man' whose farm yielded such heavy crops that he decided to build new and larger barns, saying, 'There will I bestow all my fruits and my goods. And I will say to my soul, Soul, thou hast much goods laid up for many years; take thine ease, eat, drink and be merry.' But God said to him, 'Thou fool, this night thy soul shall be required of thee.' And it was so. At the height of his prosperity, he died.

Think of this man. If he lived in our community today, he would be considered 'a big shot'. He would abound with social prestige and community respectability. He would be one of the privileged few in the economic power structure. And yet a Galilean peasant had the audacity to call him a fool.

Jesus did not call this man a fool merely because he possessed wealth. Jesus never made a sweeping indictment against wealth. Rather, He condemned the misuse of wealth. Money, like any other force such as electricity, is amoral and can be used for either good or evil. It is true that Jesus commanded the rich young ruler to 'sell all,' but in this instance, as Dr George A. Buttrick has said, Jesus was prescribing individual surgery, not making a universal diagnosis. Nothing in wealth is inherently vicious, and nothing in poverty is inherently virtuous.

Jesus did not condemn this man because he had made money in a dishonest fashion. Apparently he acquired his wealth by hard work and the practical know-how and far-sighted vision of a good businessman. Why, then, was he a fool?

I

The rich man was a fool because he permitted the ends for which he lived to become confused with the means by which he lived. The economic structure of his life absorbed his destiny. Each of us lives in two realms, the internal and the external. The internal is that realm of spiritual ends expressed in art, literature, morals and religion. The external is that complex of devices, techniques, mechanisms and instrumentalities by means of which we live. These include the house we live in, the car we drive, the clothes we wear, the economic sources we acquire – the material stuff we must have to exist. There is always a danger that we will permit the means by which we live to replace the ends for which we live, the internal to become lost in the external. The rich man was a fool because he failed to keep a line of distinction between means and ends, between structure and destiny. His life was submerged in the rolling waters of his livelihood. This does not mean that the external in our lives is not important. We have both a privilege and a duty to seek the basic material necessities of life. Only an irrelevant religion fails to be concerned about man's economic well-being. Religion at its best realizes that the soul is crushed as long as the body is tortured with hunger pangs and harrowed with the need for shelter. Jesus recognized that we need food, clothing, shelter and economic security. He said in clear and concise terms, 'Your Father knoweth what things ye have need of.' But Jesus knew that man was more than a dog to be satisfied by a few economic bones. He realized that the internal of a man's life is as significant as the external. So He added, 'Seek ye first the kingdom of God, and his righteousness; and all these things shall be added unto you.' The tragedy of the rich man was that he sought the means first, and in the process the ends were swallowed up in the means.

The richer this man became materially the poorer he became intellectually and spiritually. He may have been married, but he probably could not love his wife. It is possible that he gave her countless material gifts, but he could not give her that which she needed most, love and affection. He may have had children, but he probably did not appreciate them. He may have had the great books of the ages shelved neatly in his library, but he never read them. He may have had access to great music, but he did not listen. His eyes did not behold the majestic splendour of the skies. His ears were not attuned to the melodious sweetness of heavenly music. His mind was closed to the insights of poets, prophets and philosophers. His title was justly merited – 'Thou fool!'

II

The rich man was a fool because he failed to realize his dependence on others. His soliloquy contains approximately sixty words, yet 'I' and 'my' occur twelve times. He has said 'I' and 'my' so often that he had lost the capacity to say 'we' and 'our'. A victim of the cancerous disease of egotism, he failed to realize that wealth always comes as a result of the commonwealth. He talked as though he could plough the fields and build the barns alone. He failed to realize that he was an heir of a vast treasury of ideas and labour to which both the living and the dead had contributed. When an individual or a nation overlooks this interdependence, we find a tragic foolishness.

We can clearly see the meaning of this parable for the present world crisis. Our nation's productive machinery constantly brings forth such an abundance of food that we must build larger barns and spend more than a million dollars daily to store our surplus. Year after year we ask, 'What shall I do, because I have no room where to bestow my fruits?' I have seen an answer in the faces of millions of poverty-stricken men and women in Asia, Africa and South America. I have seen an answer in the appalling poverty in the Mississippi Delta and the tragic insecurity of the unemployed in large industrial cities of the North. What can we do? The answer is simple: feed the poor, clothe the naked and heal the sick. Where can we store our goods? Again the answer is simple: we can store our surplus food free of charge in the shrivelled stomachs of the millions of God's children who go to bed hungry at night. We can use our vast resources of wealth to wipe poverty from the earth.

All of this tells us something basic about the interdependence of men and nations. Whether we realize it or not, each of us is eternally 'in the red.' We are everlasting debtors to known and unknown men and women. We do not finish breakfast without being dependent on more than half of the world. When we arise in the morning, we go into the bathroom where we reach for a sponge which is provided for us by a Pacific Islander. We reach for soap that is created for us by a Frenchman. The towel is provided by a Turk. Then at table we drink coffee which is provided for us by a Brazilian, or tea by a Chinese, or cocoa by a West African. Before we leave for our jobs we are beholden to more than half the world.

In a real sense, all life is interrelated. All men are caught in an inescapable network of mutuality, tied in a single garment of destiny. Whatever affects one directly affects all indirectly. I can never be what I ought to be until you are what you ought to be, and you can never be what you ought to be until I am what I ought to be. This is the interrelated structure of reality.

The rich man tragically failed to realize this. He thought that he could live and grow in his little self-centred world. He was an individualist gone wild. Indeed, he was an eternal fool!

III

Jesus called the rich man a fool because he failed to realize his dependence on God. He talked as though he unfolded the seasons and provided the fertility of the soil, controlled the rising and setting of the sun, and regulated the natural processes that produce the rain and the dew. He had an unconscious feeling that he was the Creator, not a creature.

This man-centred foolishness has had a long and ofttimes disastrous reign in the history of mankind. Sometimes it is theoretically expressed in the doctrine of materialism, which contends that reality may be explained in terms of matter in motion, that life is 'a physiological process with a physiological meaning,' that man is a transient accident of protons and electrons travelling blind, that thought is a temporary product of grey matter, and that the events of history are an interaction of matter and motion operating by the principle of necessity. Having no place for God or for eternal ideas, materialism is opposed to both theism and idealism.

This materialistic philosophy leads inevitably to a dead-end street in an intellectually senseless world. To believe that human personality is

149

the result of the fortuitous interplay of atoms and electrons is as absurd as to believe that a monkey by hitting typewriter keys at random will eventually produce a Shakespeare play. Sheer magic! It is much more sensible to say with Sir James Jeans, the physicist, that 'the universe seems to be nearer to a great thought than to a great machine,' or with Arthur Balfour, the philosopher, that 'we now know too much about matter to be materialists.' Materialism is a weak flame that is blown out by the breath of mature thinking.

Another attempt to make God irrelevant is found in non-theistic humanism, a philosophy that deifies man by affirming that humanity is God. Man is the measure of all things. Many modern men who have embraced this philosophy contend, as did Rousseau, that human nature is essentially good. Evil is to be found only in institutions, and if poverty and ignorance were to be removed, everything would be all right. The twentieth century opened with such a glowing optimism. Men believed that civilization was evolving toward an earthly paradise. Herbert Spencer skilfully moulded the Darwinian theory of evolution into the heady idea of automatic progress. Men became convinced that there is a sociological law of progress which is as valid as the physical law of gravitation.

Possessed of this spirit of optimism, modern man broke into the storehouse of nature and emerged with many scientific insights and technological developments that completely revolutionized the earth. The achievements of science have been marvellous, tangible and concrete.

Witnessing the amazing advances of science, modern man exclaimed:

> Science is my shepherd; I shall not want.
> It maketh me to lie down in green pastures;
> It leadeth me beside the still waters.
> It restoreth my soul . . .
> I will fear no evil: for science is with me;
> Its rod and its staff they comfort me.

Man's aspirations no longer turned Godward and heavenward. Rather, man's thoughts were confined to man and earth. And man offered a strange parody on the Lord's Prayer: 'Our brethren which are upon the earth, hallowed be our name. Our kingdom come. Our will be done on earth, for there is no heaven.' Those who formerly turned to God to find solutions for their problems turned to science and technology, convinced that they now possessed the instruments needed to usher in the new society.

Then came the explosion of this myth. It climaxed in the horrors of Nagasaki and Hiroshima and in the fierce fury of fifty-megaton bombs. Now we have come to see that science can give us only physical power, which, if not controlled by spiritual power, will lead inevitably to cosmic doom. The words of King Alfred the Great are still true: 'Power is never a good unless it be good that has it.' We need something more spiritually sustaining and morally controlling than science. It is an instrument which, under the power of God's Spirit, may lead man to greater heights of physical security, but apart from God's Spirit, science is a deadly weapon that will lead only to deeper chaos. Why fool ourselves about automatic progress and the ability of man to save himself? We must lift up our minds and eyes unto the hills from whence cometh our true help. Then, and only then, will the advances of modern science be a blessing rather than a curse.

Without dependence on God our efforts turn to ashes and our sunrises into darkest night. Unless His Spirit pervades our lives, we find only what G. K. Chesterton called 'cures that don't cure, blessings that don't bless and solutions that don't solve.' 'God is our refuge and strength, a very present help in trouble.'

Unfortunately, the rich man did not realize this. He, like many men of the twentieth century, became so involved in big affairs and small trivialities that he forgot God. He gave the finite infinite significance and elevated a preliminary concern to ultimate standing.

After the rich man had accumulated his vast resources of wealth – at the moment when his stocks were accruing the greatest interest and his palatial home was the talk of the town – he came to that experience which is the irreducible common denominator of all men, death. The fact that he died at this particular time adds verve and drama to the story, but the essential truth of the parable would have remained the same if he had lived to be as old as Methuselah. Even if he had not died physically, he was already dead spiritually. The cessation of breathing was a belated announcement of an earlier death. He died when he failed to keep a line of distinction between the means by which he lived and the ends for which he lived and when he failed to recognize his dependence on others and on God.

May it not be that the 'certain rich man' is Western civilization? Rich in goods and material resources, our standards of success are almost inextricably bound to the lust for acquisition. The means by which we live are marvellous indeed. And yet something is missing. We have learned to fly the air like birds and swim the sea like fish, but we have not learned the simple art of living together as brothers. Our abundance has brought us neither peace of mind nor serenity of spirit. An oriental writer, Abraham Mitrie Rihbany, has portrayed our dilemma in candid terms:

You call your thousand material devices 'labour-saving machinery', yet you are for ever 'busy'. With the multiplying of your machinery you grow increasingly fatigued, anxious, nervous, dissatisfied. Whatever you have, you want more; and wherever you are you want to go somewhere else. You have a machine to dig the raw material for you . . . , a machine to manufacture [it] . . . , a machine to transport [it] . . . , a machine to sweep and dust, one to carry messages, one to write, one to talk, one to sing, one to play at the theatre, one to vote, one to sew, . . . and a hundred others to do a hundred other things for you, and still you are the most nervously busy man in the world . . . your devices are neither time-saving nor soul-saving machinery. They are so many sharp spurs which urge you on to invent more machinery and to do more business.

This is poignantly true and tells us something about Western civilization that cannot be cast aside as a prejudiced charge by an oriental thinker who is jealous of occidental prosperity. We cannot escape the indictment. The means by which we live have outdistanced the ends for which we live. Our scientific power has outrun our spiritual power. We have guided missiles and misguided man. Like the rich man of old, we have foolishly minimized the internal of our lives and maximized the external. We have absorbed life in livelihood. We will not find peace in our generation until we learn anew that 'a man's life consisteth not in the abundance of things which he possesseth,' but in those inner treasuries of the spirit which 'no thief approacheth nor moth corrupteth.'

Our hope for creative living lies in our ability to reestablish the spiritual ends of our lives in personal character and social justice. Without this spiritual and moral reawakening we shall destroy ourselves in the misuse of our own instruments. Our generation cannot escape the question of our Lord: What shall it profit a man if he gain the whole world of externals – aeroplanes, electric lights, automobiles and colour television – and lose the internal – his own soul?

4 Unfulfilled Dreams, by Dr Martin Luther King, Ebenezer Baptist Church, Atlanta, 3 March 1968

I want to preach this morning from the subject 'Unfulfilled Dreams'. My text is taken from 1 Kings 8. Sometimes it's overlooked. It is not one of the most familiar passages in the Old Testament. But I will never forget when I first came across it. It struck me as a passage having cosmic significance because it says so much in so few words about things that we all experience in life. David, as you know, was a great king. And the one thing that was foremost in David's mind and in his heart was to build a great temple. The building of the temple was considered to be the most significant thing facing the Hebrew people, and the king was expected to bring this into being. David had the desire; he started.

And then we come to that passage in the eighth chapter of 1 Kings which reads, 'And it was in the heart of David my father to build an house for the name of the Lord God of Israel. And the Lord said unto David my father, "Whereas it was in thine heart to build an house unto my name, thou didst well that it was within thine heart".' And that's really what I want to talk about this morning: It is well that it was within your heart. As if to say, 'David, you will not be able to finish the temple. You will not be able to build it. But I just want to bless you because it was in your heart. Your dream will not be fulfilled. The majestic hopes that guided your days will not be carried out in terms of an actual temple coming into being that you were able to build. But I bless you, David, because it was in your heart. You had the desire to do it; you had the intention to do it; you tried to do it; you started to do it. And I bless you for having the desire and intention in your heart. It is well that it was within your heart.'

So many of us in life start out building temples: temples of character, temples of justice, temples of peace. And so often we don't finish them. Because life is like Schubert's *Unfinished Symphony*. At so many points we start, we try, we set out to build our various temples. And I guess one of the great agonies of life is that we are constantly trying to finish that which is unfinishable. We are commanded to do that. And so we, like David, find ourselves in so many instances having to face the fact that our dreams are not fulfilled.

Now, let us notice first that life is a continual story of shattered dreams. Mahatma Gandhi laboured for years and years for the independence of his people. And through a powerful non-violent revolution he was able to win that independence. For years the Indian people had been dominated politically, exploited economically, segregated and humiliated by foreign powers, and Gandhi struggled against it. He struggled to unite his own people, and nothing was greater in his mind than to have India's one, great, united country moving towards a higher destiny. This was his dream.

But Gandhi had to face the fact that he was assassinated and died with a broken heart, because that nation that he wanted to unite ended up being divided between India and Pakistan as a result of the conflict between the Hindus and the Muslims. Life is a long, continual story of setting out to build a great temple and not being able to finish it.

Woodrow Wilson dreamed a dream of a League of Nations, but he died before the promise was delivered. The apostle Paul talked one day about wanting to go to Spain. It was Paul's greatest dream to go to

Spain, to carry the gospel there. Paul never got to Spain. He ended up in a prison cell in Rome. This is the story of life.

So many of our forebears used to sing about freedom. And they dreamed of the day that they would be able to get out of the bosom of slavery, the long night of injustice. (*Yes, sir*) And they used to sing little songs: 'Nobody knows de trouble I seen, nobody knows but Jesus.' (*Yes*) They thought about a better day as they dreamed their dream. And they would say, 'I'm so glad the trouble don't last always. (*Yeah*) By and by, by and by, I'm going to lay down my heavy load.' (*Yes, sir*) And they used to sing it because of a powerful dream. (*Yes*) But so many died without having the dream fulfilled.

And each of you this morning is in some way building some kind of temple. The struggle is always there. It gets discouraging sometimes. It gets very disenchanting sometimes. Some of us are trying to build a temple of peace. We speak out against war, we protest, but it seems that your head is going against a concrete wall. It seems to mean nothing. (*Glory to God*) And so often as you set out to build the temple of peace you are left lonesome; you are left discouraged; you are left bewildered.

Well, that is the story of life. And the thing that makes me happy is that I can hear a voice crying through the vista of time, saying: 'It may not come today or it may not come tomorrow, but it is well that it is within your heart. (*Yes*) It's well that you are trying.' (*Yes it is*) You may not see it. The dream may not be fulfilled, but it's just good that you have a desire to bring it into reality. (*Yes*) It's well that it's within your heart.

Thank God this morning that we do have hearts to put something meaningful in. Life is a continual story of shattered dreams.

Now, let me bring out another point. Whenever you set out to build a creative temple, whatever it may be, you must face the fact that there is a tension at the heart of the universe between good and evil. (*Yes, sir*) Hinduism refers to this as a struggle between illusion and reality. Platonic philosophy used to refer to it as a tension between body and soul. Zoroastrianism, a religion of old, used to refer to it as a tension between the god of light and the god of darkness. Traditional Judaism and Christianity refer to it as a tension between God and Satan. Whatever you call it, there is a struggle in the universe between good and evil.

Now, not only is that struggle structured out somewhere in the external forces of the universe, it's structured in our own lives. Psychologists have tried to grapple with it in their way and so they say various things. Sigmund Freud used to say that this tension is a tension between what he called the id and the super-ego.

But you know, some of us feel that it's a tension between God and man. And in every one of us this morning there's a war going on. (*Yes, sir*) It's a civil war. (*Yes, sir*) I don't care who you are, I don't care where you live, there is a civil war going on in your life. (*Yes it is*) And every time you set out to be good, there's something pulling you on, telling you to be evil. It's going on in your life. (*Preach it*) Every time you set out to love, something keeps pulling on you, trying to get you to hate. (*Yes. Yes, sir*) Every time you set out to be kind and say nice things about people, something is pulling on you to be jealous and envious and to spread evil gossip about them. (*Yes. Preach it*) There's a civil war going on. There is a schizophrenia, as the psychiatrists would call it, going on within all of us. And there are times when all of us know somehow that there is a Mr Hyde and a Dr Jekyll in us. And we end up having to cry out with Ovid, the Latin poet, 'I see and approve the better things of life, but the evil things I do.' We end up having to agree with Plato that the human personality is like a charioteer with two headstrong horses, each wanting to go in different directions. Or sometimes we have to end up crying out with St Augustine as he said in his *Confessions*, 'Lord, make me pure, but not yet.' (*Amen*) We end up crying out with the apostle Paul, (*Preach it*) 'The good that I would I do not; and the evil that I would not, that I do.' Or we end up having to say with Goethe that 'there's enough stuff in me to make both a gentleman and a rogue.' (*All right. Amen*) There's a tension at the heart of human nature. (*Oh yeah*) And whenever we set out to dream our dreams and to build our temples, we must be honest enough to recognize it.

And this brings me to the basic point of the text. In the final analysis, God does not judge us by the separate incidents or the separate mistakes that we make, but by the total bent of our lives. In the final analysis, God knows (*Yes*) that his children are weak and they are frail. (*Yes, he does*) In the final analysis, what God requires is that your heart is right. (*Amen. Yes*) Salvation isn't reaching the destination of absolute morality, but it's being in the process and on the right road. (*Yes*)

There's a highway called Highway 80. I've marched on that highway from Selma, Alabama to Montgomery. But I will never forget my first experience with Highway 80 was driving with Coretta and Ralph and Juanita Abernathy to California. We drove from Montgomery all the way to Los Angeles on Highway 80 – it goes all the way out to Los Angeles. And you know, being a good man, being a good woman, does not mean that you've arrived in Los Angeles. It simply means that you're on Highway 80. (*Lord have mercy*) Maybe you haven't got as far as Selma, or maybe you haven't got as far as Meridian, Mississippi, or Monroe, Louisiana – that isn't the question. The question is whether you are on the right road. (*That's right*) Salvation is being on the right road, not having reached a destination.

155

Oh, we have finally to face the point that there is none good but the Father. (*That's right*) But if you're on the right road, God has the power, (*Yes, sir*) and he has something called Grace. (*Yes, sir*) And he puts you where you ought to be.

Now the terrible thing in life is to be trying to get to Los Angeles on Highway 78. That's when you are lost. (*Yes*) That sheep was lost, not merely because he was doing something wrong in that parable, but he was on the wrong road. (*Yes*) And he didn't even know where he was going; he became so involved in what he was doing, nibbling sweet grass, (*Make it plain*) that he got on the wrong road. (*Amen*) Salvation is being sure that you're on the right road. (*Yes. Preach it*) It is well (that's what I like about it) that it was within your heart. (*Yes*)

Some weeks ago somebody was saying something to me about a person that I have great, magnificent respect for. And they were trying to say something that didn't sound too good about his character, something he was doing. And I said, 'Number one, I don't believe it. But number two, even if he is, (*Make it plain*) he's a good man because his heart is right.' (*Amen*) And in the final analysis, God isn't going to judge him by that little separate mistake that he's making, (*No, sir*) because the bent of his life is right.

And the question I want to raise this morning with you: Is your heart right? (*Yes. Preach*) If your heart isn't right, fix it up today; get God to fix it up. (*Go ahead*) Get somebody to be able to say about you, 'He may not have reached the highest height, (*Preach it*) he may not have realized all of his dreams, but he tried.' (*Yes*) Isn't that a wonderful thing for somebody to say about you? 'He tried to be a good man. (*Yes*) He tried to be a just man. He tried to be an honest man. (*Yes*) His heart was in the right place.' (*Yes*) And I can hear a voice saying, crying out through the eternities, 'I accept you. (*Preach it*) You are a recipient of my grace because it was in your heart. (*Yes*) And it is so well that it was within your heart.' (*Yes, sir*)

I don't know this morning about you, but I can make a testimony. (*Yes, sir. That's my life*) You don't need to go out this morning saying that Martin Luther King is a saint. Oh, no. (*Yes*) I want you to know this morning that I'm a sinner like all of God's children. But I want to be a good man. (*Yes. Preach it*) And I want to hear a voice saying to me one day, 'I take you in and I bless you, because you try. (*Yes. Amen*) It is well (*Preach it*) that it was within your heart.' (*Yes*) What's in your heart this morning? (*Oh Lord*) If you get your heart right . . .

Oh, this morning, if I can leave anything with you, let me urge you to be sure that you have a strong boat of faith. (*Laughter*) The winds are going to blow. (*Yes*) The storms of disappointment are coming. (*Yes*) The agonies and the anguishes of life are coming. (*Yes, sir*) And be sure

156

that your boat is strong, and also be very sure that you have an anchor. (*Amen*) In times like these, you need an anchor. And be very sure that your anchor holds. (*Yes. Glory to God*)

It will be dark sometimes, and it will be dismal and trying, and tribulations will come. But if you have faith in the God that I'm talking about this morning, it doesn't matter. (*Yes*) For you can stand up amid the storms. And I say it to you out of experience this morning; yes, I've seen the lightning flash. (*Yes, sir*) I've heard the thunder roll. (*Yes*) I've felt sin-breakers dashing, trying to conquer my soul. But I've heard the voice of Jesus, saying still to fight on. He promised never to leave me, (*Yes, sir*) never to leave me alone. (*Thank you, Jesus*) No, never alone. No, never alone. He promised never to leave me. Never to leave me alone. (*Glory to God*)

And when you get this faith, you can walk with your feet solid to the ground and your head to the air, and you fear no man. (*Go ahead*) And you fear nothing that comes before you. (*Yes, sir*) Because you know that God is even in Crete. (*Amen*) If you ascend to the heavens, God is there. If you descend to hell, God is even there. If you take the wings of the morning and fly out to the uttermost parts of the sea, even God is there. Everywhere we turn we find him. We can never escape him.

Preached one month before Martin Luther King's assassination.

Study Suggestions

1 After reading these four sermons, what is your first impression of each? Which of the four do you feel spoke to you most – and which least? (This question is of limited value because we were not there, and none of these sermons were preached for us or probably even for people like us.)

2 It may be more useful to ask of each sermon the following questions, each of which echo things said on earlier pages of this Guide:

(a) Did this sermon communicate the word of God by expounding the text of Scripture? (p. 4)

(b) Did it at some point focus on the person and work of Jesus Christ? (p. 23)

(c) Did it seem to effectively relate to the world in which the listeners lived? (pp. 9–14)

(d) Did it seem to engage with the issues and problems being faced by the listeners? (pp. 10–17)

(e) Did the illustrations clarify and illuminate the teaching being given? (pp. 20–2, 120–21)

(f) Was the opening designed to grab the attention of the hearers – and how? (pp. 28–9)

(g) Did the ending sum up the substance of the sermon? (pp. 30–31)

(h) Did the ending suggest an appropriate response to the listeners? (pp. 23, 24, 49)

(i) Was the aim of the sermon clear, and what was it? (pp. 18–19)

(j) Pick out and identify any rhetorical devices effectively used in the sermon. (Chapter 5)

(k) In what ways would the imagination and enthusiasm of the listeners be activated? (pp. 52–4)

(l) Which indirect methods listed in Chapter 4 did you find in this sermon?

(m) Was the language and content simple or complicated, easy or hard to follow? (pp. 25, 26, 50)

(n) Was it faithful to the teaching and message of the text? (Chapter 6)

(o) Did any part of the sermon strike you as specially new, true or relevant?

(p) Did the sermon raise any questions or difficulties in your mind?

THE LAST WORD

Finally, all preachers feel nervous before entering the pulpit, especially those who are new to the experience. And not only they; Martin Luther wrote, 'Although I am old and experienced in preaching, I tremble whenever I ascend the pulpit' (quoted in Morris, 1996:3). It would be very surprising if they did not feel nervous, for they are trying to do what is impossible. They are trying to 'bring . . . the news of the boundless riches of Christ . . . and to know the love of Christ that surpasses knowledge', as St Paul put it (Ephesians 3.8, 19, my translation). If it was impossible for St Paul and for Luther, it will certainly be impossible for you and me. There are, however, three Golden Rules:

1 Be yourself, for God made you and called you to proclaim his word as you are, and said 'with stammering lip and with alien tongue he will speak to this people' (Isaiah 28.11).
2 Call on the Spirit of God for his help and his enabling.
3 Remember that God has *not* called you to tell people just what to think and how to live, or to control the ways in which they serve God or to rule over a passive and obedient congregation. The Church's preachers have too often done this in the past. Better advice comes from the popular children's author, Philip Pullman:

> 'Tell them stories. That's what we didn't know. All this time, and we never knew! But they need the truth. That's what nourishes them. You must tell them true stories, and everything will be well, everything. Just tell them stories.' (*The Amber Spyglass*, p. 455)

And why? Because the truest of all stories is the story of Jesus and what he does in his people and in the world. Then 'you will know the truth', he said, 'and the truth will set you free' (John 8.32).

KEY TO STUDY SUGGESTIONS

Please note that this Key shows places where answers may be found and sometimes gives suggested answers. But other answers may be equally correct. Many of the questions have no answers except those which come from the opinions and experiences of the reader.

Chapter 1

1 (1) vv. 48–51; (2) vv. 31, 32; (3) nothing in John 6 but see 1 Cor. 10.1–4; (4) vv. 55, 56, 63; (5) John 13.1.
2 See pp. 8 and 106.
5 You could easily find answers in 1 Corinthians and Colossians, and other letters also.
6 The doctrine of the Person of Christ (vv. 6, 7); the doctrine of the Work of Christ (vv. 8, 9); the example of Christ (v. 5).
8 See p. 14.

Chapter 2

1 See Luke 1.3–4; John 20.31; 1 John 1.3–4, 5.13.
3 To help readers to recognize that God was displeased with the way they were living.
4 The writer wanted to show his readers what the Church should be like in its practical ministry.
5 See p. 27.
6 Examples are: (a) Luke 13.4; (b) Mark 12.1–12; (c) Mark 7.17–23; (d) Mark 10.23–5.
8 The first seems to be unfair to those who worked the longest. The second challenges the common belief that Pharisees were holy and tax-collectors were sinful in God's sight.
10 See pp. 4, 34 and 35.

Chapter 3

3 See pp. 22, 38, 43 and 44.
4 See p. 39.
5 See pp. 39–40.
6 He spoke in terms of Greek philosophy at Athens, and to the Colossians about their belief in spiritual powers standing between

God and themselves; he tried to encourage the Romans to think things out for themselves.

9 See pp. 43–4.

12 See pp. 23, 24, 50, 79. They aimed to teach the Bible simply, clearly and practically and to save people.

Chapter 4

1 The first story: Help the helpless and one day they will help you. The second story: Outsiders are often more responsive to God than his people. See pp. 71–2.

2 By telling a story about other people, then showing how it is true of the hearers. See Romans 2.17–23.

3 Examples might be legends about creation, human nature, offending people, death, etc.

6 Jeremiah 13, burying a loincloth: God loved his people but they abandoned him and were ruined.

Jeremiah 19, smashing a jar: God will smash the city of Jerusalem.

Jeremiah 27, bearing a yoke: God tells the people to submit to the King of Babylon.

Jeremiah 32, buying a field: God promises to restore the land and ownership of property.

Hosea 1 and 3, marrying a prostitute: Israel was unfaithful but God loved them.

9 E.g. familiar things of daily life, cleansing, end of old and start of new life, Christ's death, unity, sharing and receiving.

Chapter 5

2 Contrast (end/beginning; many/few); three-part sayings (end x 3; so x 3).

3 (a) 'I have a dream'; 'The price is high but the end is near'; 'There was no Naboth to say No!'

(b) He began by calling for freedom in the Northern states; then he called for freedom in the South, where racial discrimination was at its worst.

4 *Marana tha* (1 Corinthians 16.21); *Eli, Eli, lama sabachthani?* (Matthew 27.46) and many others.

5 Both of them identified with the people and expressed what they were feeling, suffering and hoping.

8 See pp. 90–1.

10 See Special Note F.

Chapter 6

2 Isaiah 55: Perhaps people in prison or detention.
  Matthew 2: Europeans who see Africans and others surpassing them in faith and discipleship.

3 Two examples might be blood sacrifice (unfamiliar to Europeans) and *Corban* (Mark 7.11).

4 Luke 9.50 is saying 'Don't condemn others'; 11.23 is saying 'Judge yourselves'.
  Luke 12.37 speaks of God's grace to his servants; 17.8 speaks of servants' obligation to their master.

5 Two examples are Romans 7.7–25 and 2 Corinthians 11.16–31.

9 Perhaps the third is most true to the writer's intention.

10 (a) Unfair distribution of property;
   (b) Greed;
   (c) Too big a harvest;
   (d) Forgetting the purpose of life.

11 Perhaps he most likely answer is (c).

12 See p. 105.

13 Possible examples are: easy – Mark 13.44–50; difficult – Luke 16.1–9.

14 Indirectly transforming a situation of conflict by acting generously.

17 2 and 3 seem true to the intention of the writers, but 4–7 are probably not.

18 Matthew 15.23: He gave her space to think and show how genuine was her faith.
   Mark 15.5 and John 18.9: Any claims he made at this point would have been misunderstood.
   Luke 23.9: He refused to satisfy Herod's curiosity about miracles.
   John 8.6: He showed that he came not to condemn law-breakers but to show mercy.

Chapter 7

1 See pp. 120–22. Some ideas might be: obey, respect, vote, criticize, actively participate, sometimes disobey.

2 See pp. 123–6.

3 See pp. 123–9.

5 Answers may be found in 1 Peter 2.20, 22, 23.

7 Answers may be found in Genesis 1.28, 29; 2.15, 24; 3.11, 18, 19.

Chapter 8

3 See pp. 133–5. Some ideas may be: hope; facing troubles; practical enabling; patience; encouragement from Jesus and the Scriptures.

4 She explains this on pp. 134 and 135.

5 Some ideas are: lack of resources, opposition, tiredness, delays, faults in the Church's ministry.

6 See p. 134.

7 The kingdom of God is found among the poor (Matthew 5.3 and James 2.5); Jesus leads the fight for justice (Matthew 12.18); helping the needy is helping Jesus (Matthew 25.40); the poor may be more generous than the rich (Mark 12.41–4); God's priority is to help needy people (Luke 7.22, 23; Galatians 2.10).

8 See p. 137. Both prophet and widow were hungry. God spoke to them both. The prophet gave the widow hope. She had faith and gave away her food. Both had to give something, or both would have died.

BIBLIOGRAPHY

Recommended Books

Craddock, Fred. *Preaching*. Nashville: Abingdon, 1985.

Day, David. *A Preaching Workbook*. London: SPCK Lynx, 1998.

Ireson, Gordon. *A Handbook of Parish Preaching*. Oxford: Mowbray, 1982.

Kurewa, J. W. Z. *Preaching and Cultural Identity*. Nashville: Abingdon, 2000.

Morris, Colin. *Raising the Dead*. London: HarperCollins, Fount, 1996.

Runia, Klaas. *The Sermon under Attack*. Exeter: Paternoster, 1983.

Stott, John. *I Believe in Preaching*. London: Hodder, 1982.

Wijngaards, John. *Communicating the Word of God*. Great Wakering: Mayhew-McCrimmon, 1978.

Other Books and Articles Used in this Guide

Anderson, W. B. *The Church in East Africa 1840–1974*. Dodoma: Central Tanganyika Press, 1977.

Atkinson, Max. *Our Masters' Voices*. London: Methuen, 1984.

Bailey, Kenneth. *Poet & Peasant and Through Peasant Eyes*. Grand Rapids: Eerdmans, 1983.

Bainton, Roland. *Here I Stand: A Life of Martin Luther*. New York: Mentor, 1955.

Barth, Karl. *Church Dogmatics*, vol. 1:2. Edinburgh: T. & T. Clark, 1956.

Barth, Karl. *Deliverance to the Captives*. London: SCM Press, 1961.

Baxter, Richard (1656). *The Reformed Pastor*, ed. J. T. Wilkinson, London: Epworth, 1950.

Berryman, Phillip. *Liberation Theology*. London: I. B. Tauris, 1987.

Bonhoeffer, Dietrich. *Letters and Papers from Prison*. London: Collins Fontana, 1961.

Bowen, Roger. . . . *So I Send You: A Study Guide to Mission*. London: SPCK, 1996.

Brilioth, Yngve. *Landmarks in the History of Preaching*. London: SPCK, 1950.

Brueggemann, Walter. *Abiding Astonishment*. Louisville: Westminster, 1991.

Brueggemann, Walter. *The Bible and Postmodern Imagination*. London: SCM Press, 1993.

Brueggemann, Walter. Lecture at St John's College, Nottingham, 1987.

Buttrick, David. *Homiletic*. London: SCM Press, 1987.

Buttrick, David. *A Captive Voice: The Liberation of Preaching*. Louisville: Westminster, 1994.

Church Mission Society video: *In the Same Boat: Church and People in Kenya*, 1991.

Clark, Kenneth. *Civilisation*. London: BBC, 1969.

Coomes, Anne. *Festo Kivengere: A Biography*. Eastbourne: Monarch, 1990.

Cranfield, C. E. B. *Commentary on St Mark*. Cambridge: CUP, 1977.

Cranfield, C. E. B. *On Romans*. Edinburgh: T. & T. Clark, 1998.

Day, David. 'Preaching the Epistles', *Anvil*, 14(4), 1997.

Donovan, Vincent. *Christianity Rediscovered*. London: SCM Press, 1978.

Dube, Musa. *Other Ways of Reading: African Women and the Bible*. Geneva: WCC, 2001.

Ebeling, Gerhard. *The Nature of Faith*. London: Collins Fontana, 1961.

Faith in the City, London: Church House Publishing, 1985.

Freire, Paulo. *Pedagogy of the Oppressed*. Harmondsworth: Penguin, 1972.

Gitari, David. *In Season and out of Season*. Oxford: Regnum, 1996.

Gitari, David. *Let the Bishop Speak*. Nairobi: Uzima, 1988.

Gitari, D. and Knighton, B. 'On Being a Christian Leader', *Transformation*, 18(4), 2001.

Goldingay, John. 'Interpreting Scripture', *Anvil*, 1(2), 1984.

Goldingay, John. 'In Preaching be Scriptural', *Anvil*, 14(2), 1997.

Haleblian, Krikor. 'Art, Theology and Contextualization: The Armenian Experience', *Missiology*, 32(3), 2004.

Harding, John. Extract from *The Ecclesiastical Sausage Machine*. BBC TV.

Haslam, William. *From Death into Life*. Marshall, Morgan & Scott, 1880.

Jackman, Stuart. *The Davidson Affair*. London: Faber, 1966.

Jenkins, P. *The Next Christendom: The Coming of Global Christianity*. Oxford: OUP, 2002.

Keck, Leander. *The Bible in the Pulpit*. Nashville: Abingdon, 1978.

King, Martin Luther Jr. *A Knock at Midnight*. London: Little, Brown & Co, 1999.

King, Martin Luther Jr. *Strength to Love*. London: Collins Fontana, 1969.

King, Roberta. 'Towards a Discipline of Christian Ethnomusicology', *Missiology*, 32(3), 2004.

Knox, John. *The Integrity of Preaching*. London: Epworth, 1957.

Kyle, Sharon. 'Truly, Madly, Deeply: Women's Experience of Preaching', *Anvil*, 14(4), 1997.

Lowry, E. *How to Preach a Parable: Designs for Narrative Sermons*. Nashville: Abingdon, 1989.

Maltby, R. *Obiter Scripta*. London: Epworth, 1952.

Manson, Peter. *Using the Bible in Preaching*. Swindon: Bible Society, 1984.

Maung Shwe Wa. *Burma Baptist Chronicle*. Rangoon: Burma Baptist Convention, 1963.

Mitchell, H. H. *The Recovery of Preaching*. London: Hodder, 1977.

Morris, Colin. Lecture delivered in Lenton, Nottingham, 1995.

Muhando, Daudi. *Hadithi za Kiafrika Zimekuwa za Kikristo*. London: SPCK, 1962.

Newbigin, Lesslie. *The Light has Come: An Exposition of the Fourth Gospel*. Grand Rapids: Eerdmans, 1982.

Norrington, D. C. *To Preach or not to Preach*. Carlisle: Paternoster, 1996.

Nouwen, Henri. *The Return of the Prodigal Son*. London: Darton, Longman & Todd, 1994.

Okri, Ben. *New Internationalist*, 2004, August.

Pascal, Blaise. *Lettres Provinciales*. London: Longmans Green, 1920.

Peel, John. *Religious Encounter and the Making of the Yoruba*. Indiana University, 2000.

Plato. *Phaedrus*. Trans. R. Hackforth, Cambridge: CUP, 1972.

Ramachandra, V. and Peskett, H. *The Message of Mission*. Leicester: IVP, 2003.

Richard, Ramesh. *Scripture Sculpture*. Grand Rapids: Baker, 1995.

Ross, Kenneth. 'The Voice of the Church in Malawi', *African Affairs*, 103 (410), 2004.

Rowling, J. K. *Harry Potter and the Philosopher's Stone*. London: Bloomsbury, 1997.

Sanneh, Lamin. *Translating the Message: The Missionary Impact on Culture*. New York: Orbis, 1989.

Smyth, Charles. *The Art of Preaching*. London: SPCK, 1940.

Stacey, John. *Preaching Reassessed*. London: Epworth, 1980.

Stuart, James. *The Interpretation of Scripture*. London: SCM Press, 1961.

Sugirtharajah, R. S. *Voices from the Margin*. New York: Orbis, 1991.

Sundkler, Bengt. *Christian Ministry in Africa*. London: SCM Press, 1960.

Sundkler, B. and Steed C. *A History of the Church in Africa*. Cambridge: CUP, 2000.

Taylor, Barbara Brown. *The Preaching Life*. Cambridge, Mass.: Cowley, 1993.

Taylor, W. E. *African Aphorisms*. London: SPCK, 1891.

Thiselton, A. 'Understanding the Word of God', in J. Stott (ed.), *Obeying Christ in a Changing World*, vol. 1, London: Hodder, 1977.

Thiselton, A. *The First Epistle to the Corinthians*. Grand Rapids: Eerdmans, 2000.

van Spanje, T. 'Contextualization', *Bulletin of John Rylands Library*, 80(1), 1998.

Walker, Carol. 'The Rhetoric of Scripture and Preaching', in R. Dodaro and G. Lawless, *Augustine and His Critics: Essays in Honour of Gerald Bonner*. London: Routledge, 2002.

Walls, A. F. *The Cross-Cultural Process*. New York: Orbis, 2002.

Wilder, Amos. *Early Christian Rhetoric*. London: SCM Press, 1964.

Wolf, Miroslav. *Exclusion and Embrace*. Nashville: Abingdon, 1996.

Printed and bound by CPI Group (UK) Ltd, Croydon, CR0 4YY

13/04/2025

14656473-0005